Pyrography Handbook

STEPHEN POOLE

First published 1997 by
Guild of Master Craftsman Publications Ltd,
166 High Street, Lewes,
East Sussex, BN7 1XU

Reprinted 1998

Front cover photograph by Zul Mukhida

ISBN 1 86108 061 1

This edition is a revised and condensed version
of *The Complete Pyrography*, published 1995 by
Guild of Master Craftsman Publications Ltd.

Designed by Ian Hunt Design

Set in Meridien

Colour separation by Viscan Graphics, Singapore

Printed in Hong Kong by H & Y Printing Ltd

CONTENTS

ACKNOWLEDGEMENTS

MY THANKS GO TO:

The late Eddie Chapleo for encouragement early on; Copford Cricket Club; Liz Mullen; Nan Taylor; Ron Bussey; The Dedham Art Centre; Roy Child; and all the suppliers of pyrographic equipment and materials, namely Peter Child & Co., Janik Enterprises Ltd and Copford Woodcraft Kitchens.

NOTE:

Throughout this book, photocopies of illustrations are recommended as sources for pyrographed designs. Unauthorized copying of copyright material is illegal. You must always check the copyright status of any work you wish to copy and use. This is especially important if you intend to sell your work.

INTRODUCTION

The term pyrography was originally coined by the Victorians from the Greek words *pur,* meaning fire, and *graphos,* meaning writing. As a craft or an art form it is available to anyone wishing to have a go, and there is no need for formal art training to achieve pleasing results. Many students are quite surprised how quickly they grasp the techniques involved, and go on to produce excellent work.

The craft has the added advantage that none of the equipment required is sophisticated, costly or difficult to use. I used a hot-wire machine for all the projects in this book other than the sampler on pages 40 to 46, and the bowl in Chapter 11. However, all the projects can be done using a solid-point pyrography tool, with the exception of the caravan project in Chapter 12. If you are using a Janik G4 solid-point machine, the best points to use for the projects are the B21, equivalent to the standard hot-wire point, and the B24, equivalent to the hot wire spoon point. If you are not using Janik or Peter Child equipment, you need to use a heated round-ended point similar in size to the tip of an average ball-point pen.

This eagle, and the men by the fire shown on page 2, were created by a gentleman in Norfolk who used heated pieces of metal to extremely good, if crude, effect.

1
MATERIALS

Although pyrography can be applied to virtually any surface that can be burned or charred, I have found that wood offers the best results, both in variety of texture, and practicability. Wood has the added advantage of being a raw material that can be either turned on a lathe or carved into a multitude of shapes and objects.

WHAT KIND OF WOOD?

A light-coloured wood will show off your work at its best, bringing out more of the detail and fine textures. However, not all such woods are suitable as some are very grainy. Pine, for example, is cheap to buy and burns well, but the difference in texture between the grain and the actual 'meat' of the wood is so great that it is difficult to burn a continuous line when passing the point of the pyrography pencil through the grain. As a result it is only suitable for subjects that require a minimum of detail.

Oak is also unsuitable. Although it is light in colour and one of the most durable woods, its grain is so hard that it almost refuses to burn at all.

Fig 1.1 Various sycamore blanks.

SYCAMORE AND OTHER SUITABLE WOODS

Sycamore has traditionally been used in the manufacture of kitchen utensils such as wooden spoons, spatulas and breadboards (see Fig 1.1). Unlike pine, it has no characteristic odour or taste, and the surface is far more friendly to the sharpened cutting edge of an expensive knife. It is also an ideal wood for pyrography, partly because of its light colour, but mainly because of the extremely small difference in hardness between the grain parts and the non-grain parts, making it easy to pyrograph.

Other suitable woods are horse chestnut, holly, boxwood, lime and English or Canadian maple. Another material I have used in vast quantities for my pyrography is known as birch-faced plywood.

BIRCH-FACED PLYWOOD

Whilst not available from your local DIY store, this material can be obtained from the larger trade suppliers in 8 x 4ft (2.44 x 1.22m) sheets. Always ask for offcuts, but if you have to buy a complete sheet, the supplier will normally be able to cut it down into more manageable pieces.

Birch-faced ply is identical to sycamore in appearance, and when sanded will give a very smooth, white surface on which to pyrograph (see Fig 1.2). The grain reacts to the pyrography tool in almost exactly the same way as the rest of the wood, just like sycamore.

Fig 1.2 Birch-faced ply.

The only difference between the two woods, from a pyrographer's point of view, is that birch-faced ply is softer and cheaper. This makes it unsuitable for pyrography blanks such as spoons, as it is far too soft, but ideal for flat illustration, and a picture or design on a thin gauge of birch-faced ply can easily be framed in the usual way.

Because birch-faced ply is so similar to sycamore, it is always useful to have a scrap with you when you are working as a means of testing for the correct temperature just before you apply the tool to the actual wood you intend to pyrograph. You may decide to cut a sheet of ply to the dimensions of your regular work area so that you always have a 'tester' readily to hand.

VENEERS

A veneer is a controlled shaving from a piece of prepared wood (see Fig 1.3). Using veneers can be an inexpensive way to experiment with a wide variety of wood surfaces. A veneer can be adhered to hardboard or cheap plywood by using a contact adhesive, giving you a more solid work area. Decorative veneers are usually approximately 0.6mm ($^{1}/_{42}$in) thick and have been used by carpenters and cabinetmakers for centuries.

Larger veneer suppliers will normally stock up to 100 different woods in veneer form. By no means all will be suitable for pyrography, but I suggest you buy a 'veneer collectors set' or sampler, which contains around 50 wood

Fig 1.3 A selection of veneers.

types, labelled with basic information including trade and botanical names, common names and country of origin.

TYPES OF VENEER

YEW

Yew is a very hard wood, which means it takes longer to make marks but enables you to produce more detailed work. Most yew is rather dark, but you can find areas of lighter wood near the bark. Yew turns very well on a lathe and has a beautiful, smooth touch when sanded.

HORSE CHESTNUT

Horse chestnut is similar in colour to sycamore but has a less pronounced grain, making it a good choice for illustrations where a minimum of grain interference is needed. It is a little softer than sycamore, but this helps in the forming of deeper grooves for texturing.

BIRD'S EYE MAPLE

I have seen pieces of this wood so beautifully marked that they should have been framed and exhibited just as they were! The surface pyrographs well, though you have to avoid the larger 'pebble' markings which characterize it, as they have a tendency to burn in a different and inconsistent way.

PEAR

This is normally a fairly dark wood, but it sands to a very smooth finish. Like horse chestnut, the grain markings offer very little resistance to the pyrography tool. However, your work will have to be more heavily burned to give you the contrast you need against the darkness of the wood.

It is worth noting that the above descriptions of how these woods behave are based on my own experiences with specific pieces of material. No two pieces of wood are ever identical; you will gain the best experience by trying the various woods yourself.

USING GRAIN MARKINGS AND BLEMISHES

Unlike the pages of a sketch pad, wood surfaces vary a great deal – even pieces cut from the same sheet of plywood. However, you will often be able to put to good use the natural grain markings of woods such as sycamore, maple and birch. Even large knots and other imperfections can usually, with a little imagination, be incorporated into your work. I have been able to make a natural marking look like a twig or branch, for example. Sometimes, a particularly interesting blemish has inspired and helped to compose an entire picture.

Apart from the recognized suppliers of blanks, you could also try kitchen reject shops, which usually have a section displaying mass-produced wooden kitchenware, often made from beech (see Fig 1.4). While such items (breadboards, chopping boards, spoons etc.) have not been made intentionally for the pyrographer, they are good surfaces on which to work. Beech is harder and darker than sycamore, with a slightly pinkish hue. You should also bear in mind that objects such as breadboards are often made from more than one piece of wood, and unless you know the type of adhesive used it is best not to burn through any of these joints.

If you know a local hobbyist woodturner, you can always approach them with an offer to buy blanks. Always keep a watchful eye open at car boot sales for old wooden items such as boxes and turned pieces, which can be rubbed down if painted and then used as blanks. You may also find that scraps of driftwood washed up by the tide will provide you with inspiration (these have often been smoothed by the sea and bleached by the sun, making their surface ideal for pyrographing).

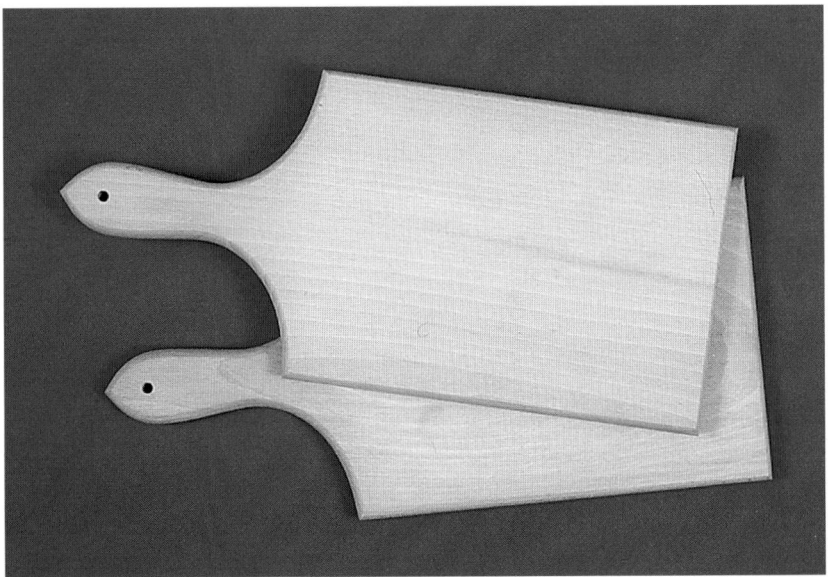

Fig 1.4 Beech cheese boards.

2
SOURCES FOR COMPOSITION

Always be on the lookout for reference material for compositions, particularly if you receive a request for a particular subject. There are various places where you can look for such material with a view to creating your own reference library. (Before reading on, please refer to the note on page vi concerning copyright.)

please refer to the note on page vi concerning copyright.

PLACES TO LOOK

Old books and magazines can be treasure troves of good quality images. Libraries are an obvious source, especially if you locate composition material for a particular specialist subject. Car boot sales are one of the best hunting grounds – you may even find old Victorian

Fig 2.1 Weldon's 'Sixpenny Series' magazines – a useful source of designs and illustrations for pyrographers.

crafts magazines and books, such as Weldon's 'Sixpenny Series' magazine (see Fig 2.1). Such publications covered a wide range of interesting crafts and provided highly adaptable illustrations and plans.

THE IMPORTANCE OF PHOTOCOPYING

It is always worth photocopying designs or illustrations that you have used or think you might use in the future. This is not only because you might mislay the original; if you trace directly through the original enough times a design will become worn and possibly difficult to replace.

All photocopying results in some loss of detail, particularly when copying colour photographs or prints. Therefore, if you can, keep the original and attach it to your photocopy. After you have used the photocopy-tracing method a few times, this loss of detail is actually an advantage. A bad photocopy makes a good plan to work from, without including lots of detail which can in any case be added later by eye. Most libraries have their own photocopying facilities, which can be useful if you plan to use their reference section for source material.

Before copying anything, always check with the librarian that you are not infringing any copyright.

CREATING A REFERENCE LIBRARY

This will save you a great deal of time doing research in libraries and so on. Magazine cuttings and photocopies can be stored in an inexpensive expanding filing wallet – the bigger the better.

I have built up a separate reference library over the years of my own photography. I like to work from my own pictures, especially on commissions and wildlife subjects, which are a particular favourite of mine.

CONCLUSION

Never throw anything away that might contain a useful pictorial reference without checking it first. There is no shortage of material, and if you collect, organize and file it properly you stand a better chance of having to hand exactly what you need when you need it.

3
TOOLS AND EQUIPMENT

There are three types of pyrography tool available.

SOLDERING-IRON TYPE

Usually German or British manufactured, this tool is inexpensive but limited in its uses. It works on the same principle as the soldering iron, the working point being heated by a cylindrical element or coil contained in the working end of the tool. A variety of interchangeable points can be fitted into the holder and secured by a screw. The disadvantages are that the whole tool soon becomes very hot and uncomfortable to handle, and, with the expansion of the hot metal, the points are difficult to keep in place. Worst of all, you have no real facility for adjusting the temperature of the point.

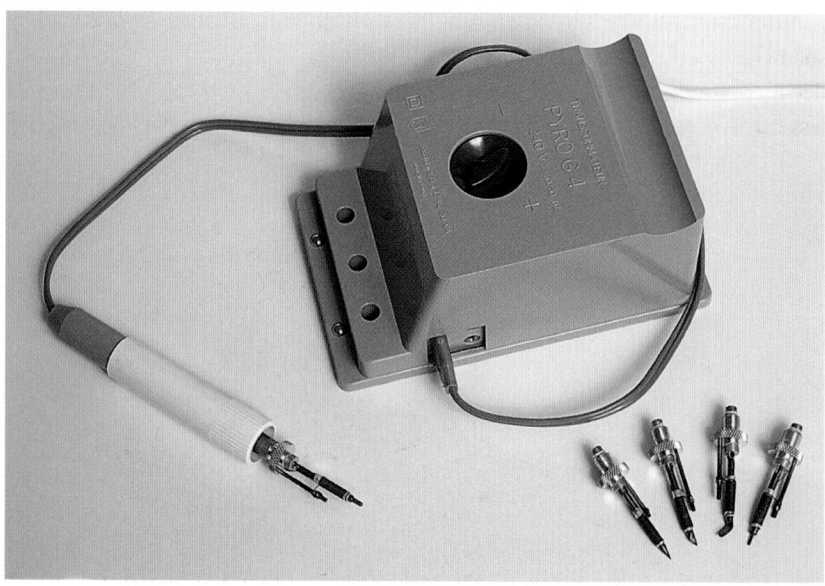

Fig 3.1 A Janik G4 solid-point machine.

SOLID-POINT TYPE

This type of tool uses solid working points which have their own miniature heating element close to the tip. This machine remains by far the most popular type of pyrography tool (see Fig 3.1).

Solid-point machines represent a substantial progression from the soldering-iron machines. A good selection of points is available in a wide variety of shapes, sizes and brands. Such machines are especially suited to the pyrographer wishing to specialize in bold pattern and repeat pattern designs. The flat-ended points are extremely efficient when large areas of uniform shading or pure black are needed.

'Brands' are specifically-shaped solid points and are a useful decorating tool, especially for the less confident, as they enable you to brand patterns easily by repeating each burn. They produce variations on a few basic shapes, such as circles, triangles and squares, and provide a huge scope for design when used imaginatively. Many skilled pyrographers produce remarkably detailed work using this very popular tool.

HOT-WIRE TYPE

This tool has a flexible point or nib made from a short length of nickel chromium wire and held between two terminals fitted to the end of a pencil or holder (see Figs 3.2 and 3.3). The working voltage of the hot-wire tool can be much lower than the soldering-iron type, and the heat of the point is capable of fine adjustment through a control box. This is my preferred working tool, which I have used for most of the projects in

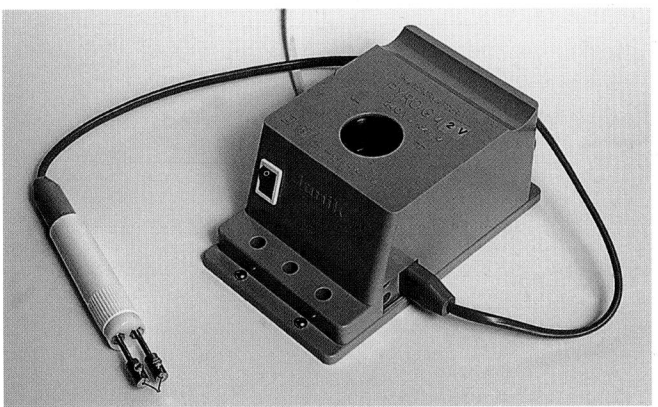

Fig 3.2 A Janik G4HW hot-wire pyrography machine.

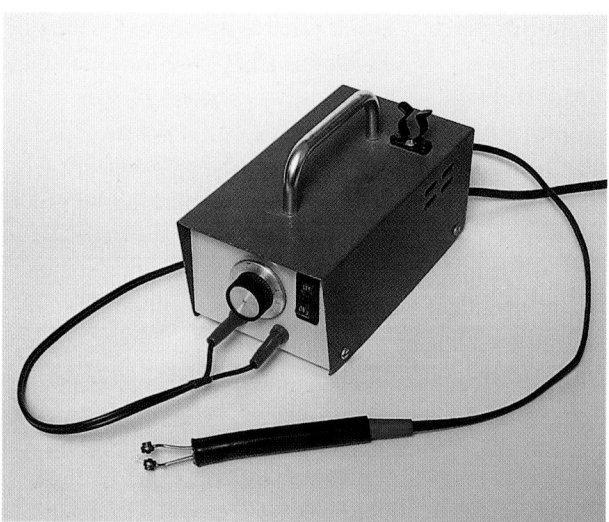

Fig 3.3 A Peter Child hot-wire pyrography machine.

this book, but they are all possible with a solid point (with the exception of the caravan in Chapter 12).

Another type of point which can be used on the hot-wire machine is the spoon point. These are simply wire points shaped at the end into a spoon shape by the application of a sharp blow with a tiny round steel punch (see page 19). It is also possible to make your own brands shaped from wire for decorative and repeat patterns.

TOOLS FOR USERS OF HOT-WIRE PYROGRAPHY MACHINES

PLIERS

These are used in the manufacture of wire points, or for adapting

points for different kinds of work with a hot-wire machine (see pages 16-20).

SMALL ANVIL

You could go out and buy a small anvil, but a large hammer head or lump hammer head will suffice.

WIRE CUTTERS

These are for accurately cutting the lengths of wire for use as points (see page 13).

SMALL SCREWDRIVER

This is for loosening and tightening the screws and clamps holding the points in place on hot-wire machines (see page 13).

ANGLEPOISE LAMP

Whatever the availability of natural light in your workspace, you will need a form of Anglepoise lamp to see clearly what you are doing. Lamps also help to highlight the tiny shadows formed in the grooves of the pyrograph, when set at an angle to the work.

PENCILS

You will need a small selection of hard and soft pencils. B or 2B is recommended for soft pencil work such as sketching or drawing on the wood surface. These are then easily rubbed off after pyrographing if they have not been completely burned away, and do not leave any indentation in the wood as a hard pencil would. Use a hard pencil for tracing. 2H to 4H are recommended. They stay sharp for a long time and give a continuous, accurate fine trace line.

PENCIL SHARPENER AND SCALPEL

Pencil sharpeners cast in metal are the best. Scalpels can be obtained from various suppliers to the hobby trade, model shops or printers' suppliers. Ask for blade 10A, which will fit the no. 3 scalpel handle. The 10A has a fine point and is very sharp.

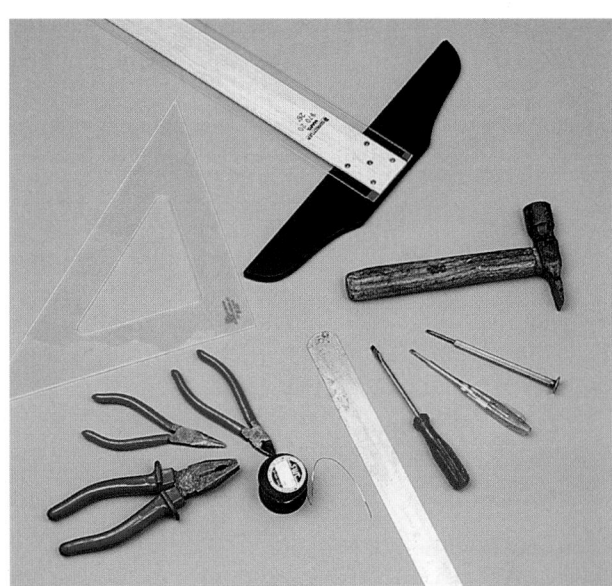

Fig 3.4 Tools required by users of hot-wire pyrography machines, including a hammer, screwdrivers, pliers, nickel chromium wire and wire cutters.

Scalpels are used to remove minor errors such as lines continued too far, highlights burnt in by mistake and so on, which can be scraped away with the scalpel.

SOFT WHITE RUBBER

This is used to remove any surplus marks and lines from the initial plan pencilled onto the wood. Use a putty rubber on black or pencil carbon marks in cases where a mark has been made too heavily and requires toning down, but not outright removal.

BROWN MASKING TAPE

Used for adhering photocopies or design plans to the wood surface. Masking tape is less likely to leave gum marks or stains on the wood than Sellotape.

BLACK PENCIL CARBON PAPER

The best type is that once commonly used to make copies of typed documents. This is now less readily available due to changes in technology but can still be found. An alternative is black ink carbon paper, which is not so good but works reasonably well. Never use blue carbon; the traces are very hard to remove.

STEEL RULER

A steel ruler is particularly useful if you have to pyrograph an accurate straight line. Using an ordinary point you can steer along the ruler on a low heat setting to make a groove that can then easily be followed with a hotter point.

Fig 3.5 General accessories for the pyrographer, including a scalpel, black pencil carbon paper, fine sandpaper, a soft rubber, pencils, sable brushes, masking tape and an Anglepoise lamp.

Plastic set square or small T-square

Very useful for centring designs onto a surface.

Sandpaper

This is needed primarily for smoothing the wood surface before beginning, although good-quality blanks are often smooth enough to work on without sanding. However, I always make it a rule to sand the wood with fine sandpaper before commencing tracing or pyrography, to ensure the surface has been studied. Fine paper will not roughen the surface, and this operation gives me the chance to observe grain markings and imperfections which will influence which way up the wood will face and where the design will be placed. A piece of corduroy is very useful at this stage for wiping off any particles of sanded wood that cannot be removed by blowing or brushing.

Sable brushes

If you intend to add colour to your work, you will need a small selection of sable brushes. These are expensive but there is no real substitute for their quality (see Fig 3.6). Two or three from size 0 upwards are sufficient. As you are only likely to use water-based paints, your brushes will be easy to clean and will last a very long time with the right care, proving a very worthwhile investment.

Fig 3.6 A selection of sable brushes.

4
STARTING OUT

CONSTRUCTING WIRE POINTS

If you decide to use a hot-wire pyrography tool you will need to know how to construct a wire point correctly. A well-made wire point will enable you to use the tool to its best advantage and produce a huge variety of textures and tones.

CONSTRUCTING A STANDARD WIRE POINT

There are four grades of Nichrome wire for making points: 26SWG (finest), 25SWG, 24SWG and 23SWG (thickest). These are obtainable from specialist suppliers.

Generally speaking, everything can be done with one gauge, and the best one to use is 24SWG. Figs 4.1–4.7 show in detail how to make such a point.

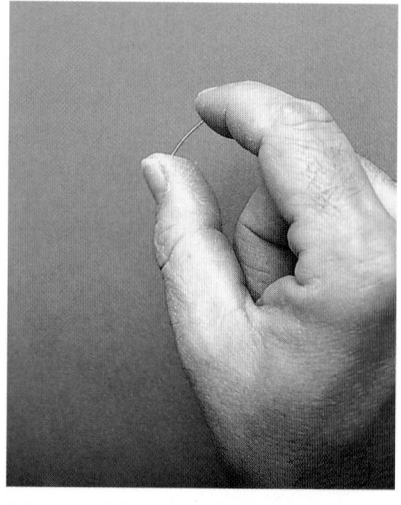

Fig 4.1 With a pair of pliers or wire cutters, cut a piece of 24SWG wire, approximately ³⁄₄in (19mm) long.

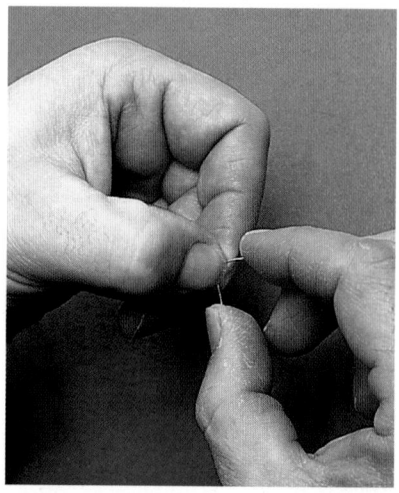

Fig 4.2 Use the ball of your forefinger and thumb to . . .

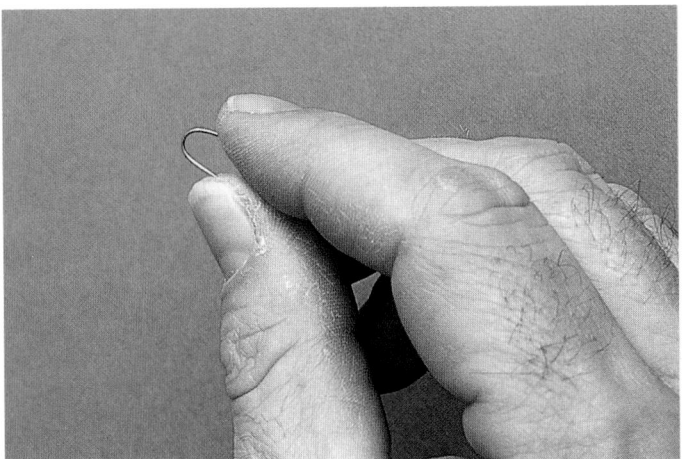

Fig 4.3 . . . bend the wire into a U-shape.

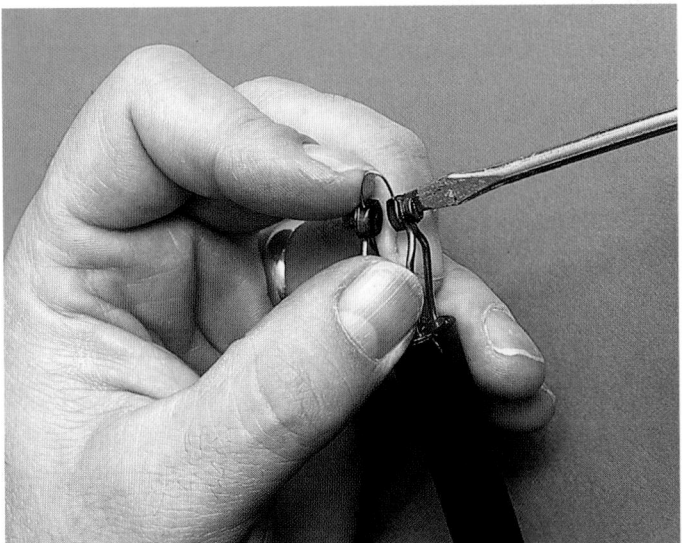

Fig 4.4 Loosen the screws on the pyrography pencil sufficiently to allow the ends of the wire to slide between the prongs and the retaining grommets. Then tighten the screws, being careful to avoid bending the prongs together. To produce a good range of marks and textures, you will need to exert a reasonable amount of pressure on the point, and so, the shorter the point the less likely it is to bend under such pressure. Manufacturer's recommendations vary, but in my own experience I have found a point length of ³⁄₈in (10mm) of wire, once tightened into position, produces very good results.

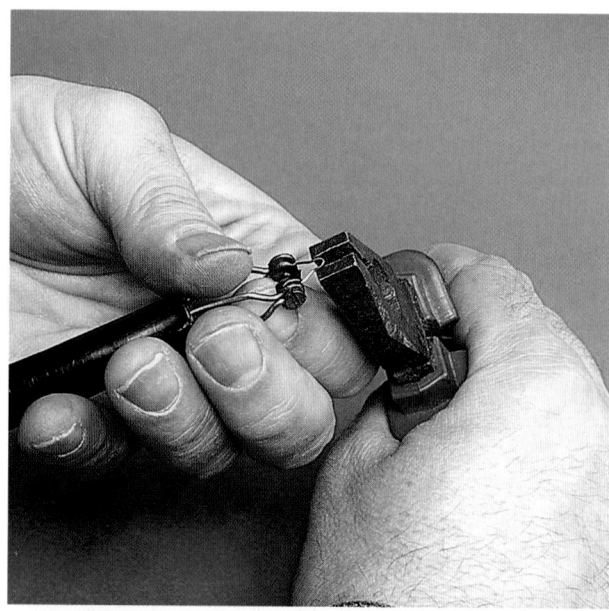

Fig 4.5 Use a pair of pliers to pinch the loop approximately halfway down to form a second loop.

Fig 4.6 Pinch the wire completely together as near to the end of the second loop as possible.

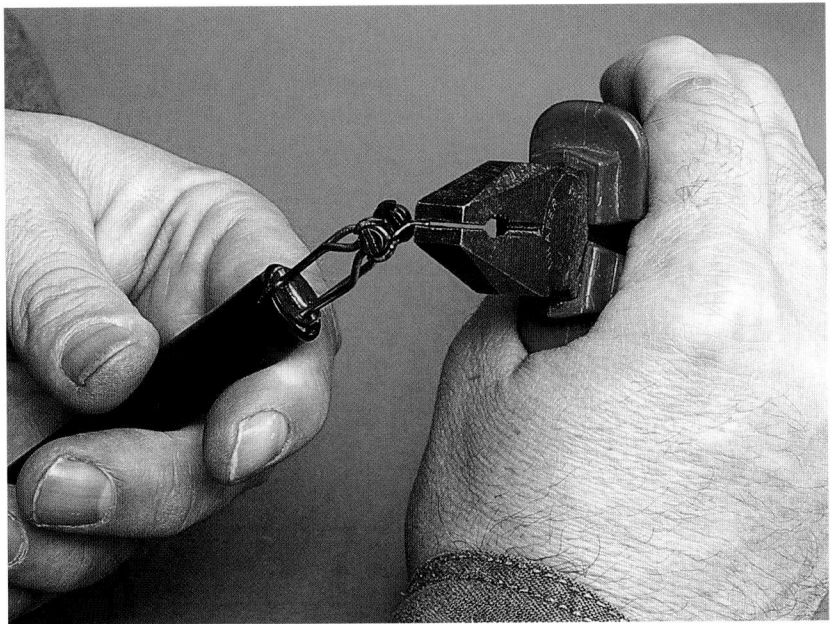

Fig 4.7 Gently bend the point with the pliers until it slopes at a comfortable angle to the work surface.

CONSTRUCTING OTHER KINDS OF POINT

Spoon points can be bought ready-made (see Fig 4.8). They can also be made quite easily by taking a standard wire point and hammering it out flat on a hard metal anvil such as the head of a hammer held in a vice. Any sharp edges can be removed by rubbing on abrasive paper. If you have a hot-wire machine but still need to burn deep, dark areas (for, say, house signs or decorative and repeat patterns) you can make your own brands of point from nickel chromium wire.

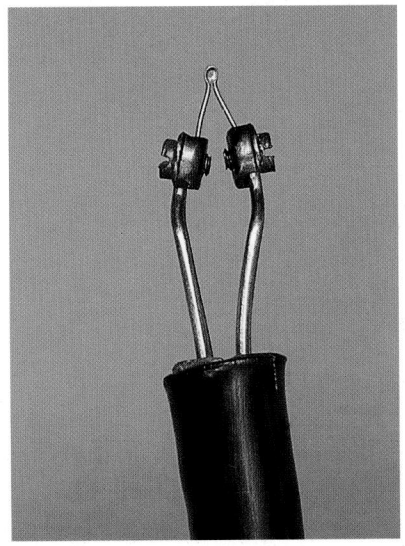

Fig 4.8 A spoon point.

Heavy gauge wire such as 24 or 23SWG should be used for rigidity. Form the brands using small pointed pliers – accuracy is important here so that the whole of the pattern surface touches evenly in use. The tool is usually held in a vertical position for branding. Alternatively, if you have a solid-point tool as well, this is even more suited to such work.

Before you actually put pen to wood, there are a number of factors which need to be addressed, including safety, surface preparation, lighting and setting the temperature of the point.

SAFETY

Modern pyrography is a very safe craft providing you observe simple safety measures. The following apply to most types of pyrography machine:

- Do not open the case of the power unit. Live terminals are exposed inside.
- Do not attempt to service the power unit without expert knowledge.
- Do not allow children to poke anything into the ventilation slots in the case.
- While the creation of much smoke is unusual, you can use a fan to dispel fumes from the wood. These may cause irritation over long sessions of work. Fans with carbon filters are ideal.
- Do not twist or bend the flex at the end of the tool or the strands of wire inside the insulation will eventually break.
- Do not wind the flex around the handle when storing the pencil.
- Do not use the control unit to power any other appliance. It has a very low voltage AC output. The pencil will not work on 12 volts or any other transformer.
- Be aware that the front panel may get hot in use. This is quite normal and depends on the heat control setting.
- Always protect the unit from damp and rain.

SAFETY FOR HOT-WIRE USERS

- Do not let the pencil terminals touch each other, short out against a metal object or touch the case of the control unit. If it is subjected to short circuits for any length of time it is liable to be permanently damaged.
- Never let the hot wire anywhere near the mains cable. If children are using the machine keep the

cable clear of the work area at all times.

- Wire points get very hot and could potentially start a fire. Stow the pencil in the clip on the power unit rather than putting it down on the bench. Always supervise inexperienced users, never leave the machine unattended and switch it off after use.

- The wires used to make the point must not be *too* short, although the shorter the point, the greater the pressure that can be exerted upon it without bending the wire. Different machines have different attachments, and you should always follow individual manufacturer's instructions concerning the recommended length of the wires for the point. In my experience, a finished point about ³⁄₈in (10mm) from the terminal gives excellent results.

- Avoid bending the terminal support struts, which are of delicate design in order to reduce heat flow to the handle.

- From time to time, dismantle the pencil terminals and clean off any tarry deposits, which will help to cure bad contacts. Oven cleaner is ideal for this, but be careful not to let it touch the handle or get inside the pencil.

PREPARING THE SURFACE OF THE WOOD

You should not need to sand good quality birch-faced ply; however, a session of gentle sanding with 180 grit paper will do no harm and gives you an opportunity to closely examine the features of the surface. Fold the paper once or twice to make it easy to grip, or wrap it round a scrap of ply. Work the paper up and down the surface in the direction of the grain using just the weight of your hand. Try to run the paper along the full length of the wood with each stroke.

Keep the sanding surface well away from the worksurface you will be using, to minimize the amount of wood and paper dust in your workspace, as these can be irritants.

You will find that sawdust on the surface of the wood will occasionally build up as you pyrograph, in the form of a carbon deposit. This will lower the temperature of the tip of the tool until the carbon detaches itself, after which the tip will heat up again. Always wipe the surface clean with a piece of corduroy cloth, which I find to be the most effective material for the job.

Finally, cut out a 1in (25mm) square of sandpaper and attach it to the top corner of the wood – this will save you having to look for a piece of sandpaper next time you want to remove carbon traces from the tip before attempting detailed work.

LIGHTING

If a light is directed across the surface being pyrographed, the minute shadows formed by the varying depths of the marks will show the overall textured effect as it is being formed. Finished pyrographs containing deeply-engraved textures take on a three-dimensional quality when displayed with the correctly angled lighting.

USING THE HOT-WIRE MACHINE

SETTING THE TEMPERATURE OF THE POINT

Once you've mastered the technique of making a good strong point, you need to find an average temperature setting and then try the point out. Hold the pencil in one hand and slowly turn the heat control dial up with the other hand. You will see that as the dial is turned, the point of the pencil soon becomes red hot (see Fig 4.9). The transformer concentrates the heat at the tip of

Fig 4.9 A red-hot point.

the point, which ensures the handle never gets hot. As soon as the tip is glowing red, turn the dial down slowly until the tip ceases to glow. You are now ready to begin.

EXERCISE

For this first exercise only two rules apply:

1 Do not 'write' with the pencil. This is a huge temptation, and is, in a way, a tribute to the equipment. The pencil is so light, it feels like a pen. So, to begin with at least, no writing.

2 Do not draw, sketch, or produce anything that can be identified. Just doodle.

Without altering the temperature setting, make a series of lines and marks. There are many ways to do this; for example, apply the point to the wood gently to produce a fine, light line (see Fig 4.10), then use a bit more pressure and move across the wood slowly to produce a broader, darker line (see Fig 4.11). A huge range of thicknesses and shades of line can be achieved, all depending on the pressure and speed applied. Experiment!

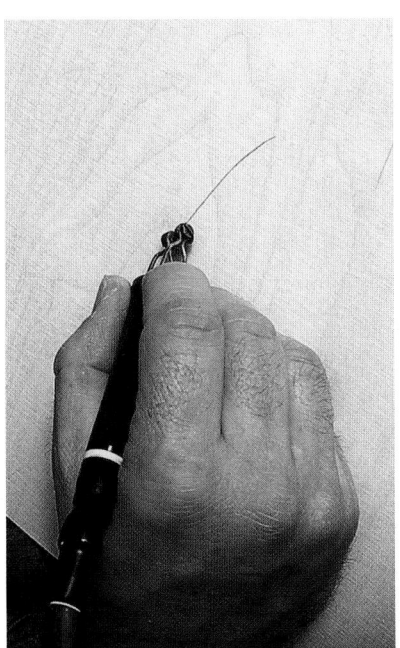

Fig 4.10 Producing a fine, light line.

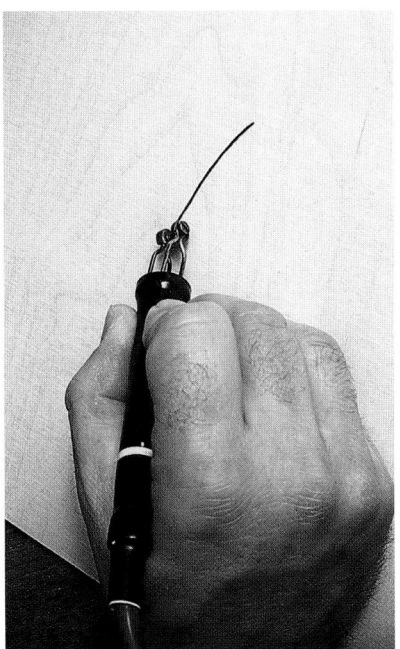

Fig 4.11 Producing a broad, dark line.

BLOBBING

By now you will have noticed that even a short line is rarely produced without 'blobbing': the line will have a blob at the start and finish (see Fig 4.12). This is because you are working with a tool that is constantly burning the wood, so any extra time it spends on any one part of a line (usually the beginning and the end) results in more burning and hence a bigger mark – a blob. Avoid this by allowing the point to arrive in contact with the wood as if it were an aircraft coming in to land, and when you get to the end of the line, let the point 'take off' again.

Don't be afraid to press hard with the point. If it bends (see Fig 4.13), turn it around and press it back into position on a piece of scrap wood. The wire is very pliable and unlikely to break.

DRAWING OR ENGRAVING?

Pyrography is a compromise between drawing and engraving, but is closer to engraving. The reproduction of *texture* is what the pyrographer is after, not just brown

Fig 4.12 'Blobbing'.

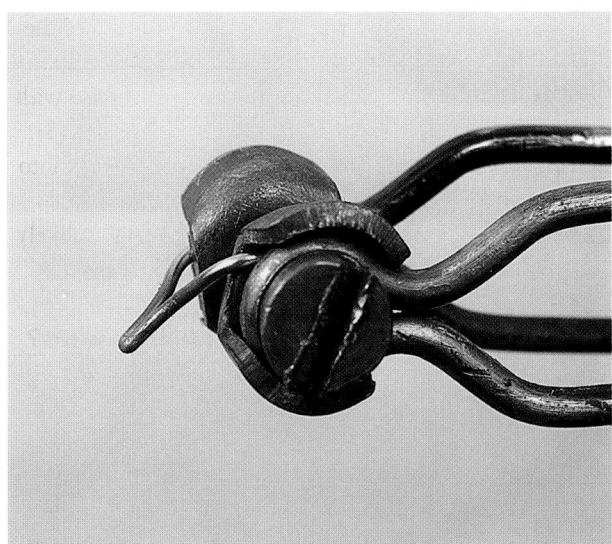

Fig 4.13 A bent point.

marks on a wooden surface. In this sense, modern pyrography tools can sometimes work against you: they are safe and simple to use and this often makes it too easy to just produce an illustration which might just as well have been done with a brown pen.

All pyrography tools are able to produce a variety of light and dark marks in a wooden surface, but much more is possible if you consider the engraving potential. Deeper pyrographed lines will create tiny shadows which collectively can suggest fur, feathers, bark, grass and a host of other tones and textures, none of which would be as easy to show using mediums such as watercolour, charcoal or pencil (see Fig 4.14).

CREATING TEXTURES

Be as imaginative as you can with your doodling. Try to group tiny areas of marks together to form different areas of texture. Try holding the pencil at different angles so that the point meets the wood at different angles. You will quickly realize that the point is far less likely to bend under pressure when applied to the wood at an angle. It is possible to cut quite deep lines into the wood by using the point slightly on its side.

See how black you can make a small area of texture. Create dots that gradually build into a cluster. Make sure each dot joins the next, and a solid dark area will result. If you want to produce a lighter

Fig 4.14 All sorts of effects, including this feather texture, are possible with the pyrography tool when it is used as an engraving device.

version of the same texture, repeat the process, but work more quickly.

You should now be able to create a good range of light and dark blobs, marks, and hopefully small areas of texture. Now try repeating some of these exercises with the temperature of the point increased. Don't, however, work with a red-hot point: at this temperature the point is more likely to bend, and will burn the wood so fast that it becomes very hard to work with any degree of accuracy.

Overburning with a hotter point than normal can produce some interesting effects. The marks you make will tend to have a 'halo' of light brown scorch marks (see Fig 4.15) around them.

USING THE SOLID-POINT MACHINE

Much of the information given so far in the chapter applies to the solid-point machine as well. The only things which do not apply are those concerning temperature setting and the problem of 'blobbing'. Set your solid-point machine at its maximum temperature, because the transformer has a larger area of metal to heat, which then cools more rapidly on contact with the surface. For the same reason, 'blobbing' just does not occur with solid-point machines.

I recommend you try the exercises described on page 23 using a Janik G4 solid-point machine, with a B21 point, which has a tip surface area very similar to that of the wire point.

CHANGING POINTS

To change the point on a hot-wire pencil, first *switch off the machine* and allow it to cool. Loosen the terminal screws, taking care not to bend the support struts. Remove the old point and replace it with a new one or a short loop of wire. Tighten the terminal screws, and if necessary squeeze the point into shape with pliers.

If you intend to do a lot of work with different points, I recommend you buy a spare pencil to hold another point.

To change the point on a solid-point pencil, switch off the machine at the mains, *allow the point to cool completely*, and replace the point in the usual way.

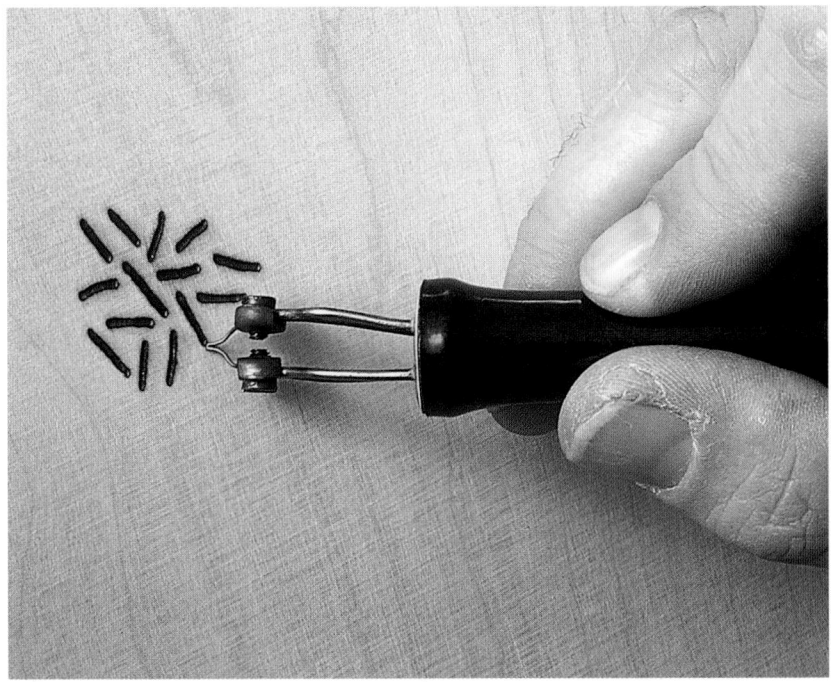

Fig 4.15 Overburning.

5
CREATING A SAMPLER

Creating a sampler is the best way to discover the potential of pyrography, and it is important that you attempt one early on. This chapter includes two samplers, with simple guidance on the way each effect was created. However, the best way to learn is to experiment. Even when you follow the simple rules I suggest here, you will find that the variety of tone and texture you can create in each square is virtually endless. Always keep any samplers you create – they are an invaluable source of future reference.

MARKING OUT THE BLANK

Take a piece of sanded birch-faced plywood 6 x 4in (152 x 102mm) or larger, and mark out a grid of 24 1in (13mm) squares using a B or 2B

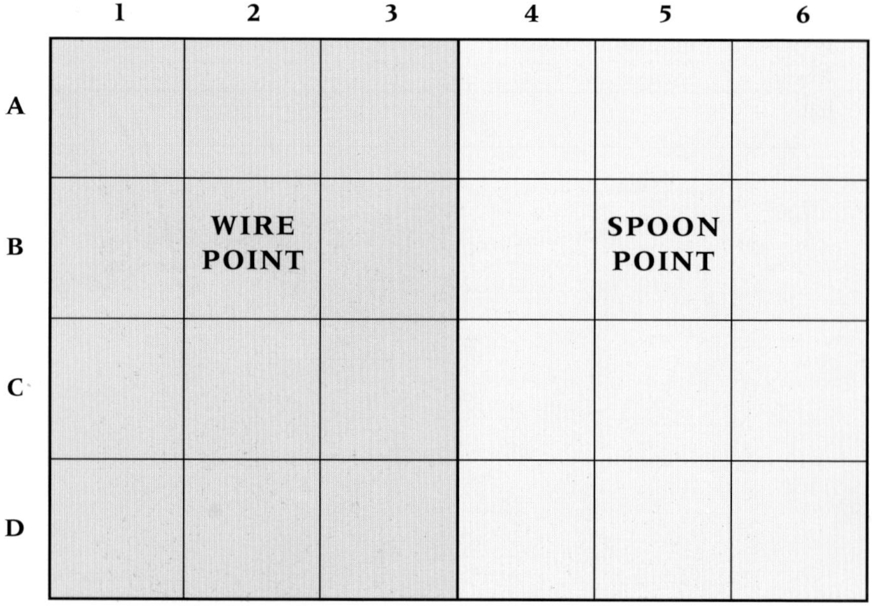

	1	2	3	4	5	6
A						
B		WIRE POINT			SPOON POINT	
C						
D						

Fig 5.1 Plan of the hot-wire sampler.

pencil (see Fig 5.1). Press very gently so that the squares are only just visible. Heavy pencil lines can mark the wood, are hard to erase, and any remaining lead can react with the pyrography tool and render the mark permanent.

HOW TO PRODUCE A SUCCESSFUL SAMPLER

▌ Make sure each square is filled completely with a different area of tone or texture.

▌ Keep each square simple, uncomplicated and *consistent*.

▌ Take your time and try to make sure each square is completely pyrographed.

▌ On at least one square, aim to produce an area of tone or texture that goes from dark to light, or vice versa.

▌ Avoid 'clever' patterns. Stick to creating textures.

▌ Produce at least one square that is as black as you can make it.

▌ Use all the variables at your disposal in terms of speed of working and heat control.

▌ When you finish a square, write down a description of how you achieved the effect, including temperature settings, pressure and technique.

MAKING A SAMPLER WITH THE HOT-WIRE TOOL

This sampler is divided into two sections. The 12 squares on the left-hand side were produced with a conventional wire point, and the 12 to the right with a spoon point (see Fig 5.2).

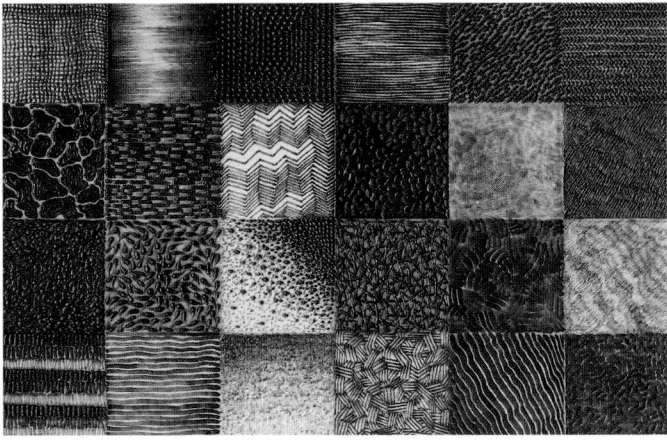

Fig 5.2 The finished sampler created with the hot-wire machine.

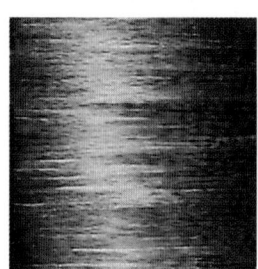

1A

Use a temperature setting that allows you to work slowly with some pressure, but is not hot enough to burn a very dark line. Start by producing a series of close lines, working *against* the grain until you have filled the square. Then repeat, reducing the temperature very slightly, working *with* the grain.

2A

Set the temperature fairly high so that the point glows pink, then reduce it a little so that the pink glow disappears. Work with the grain, applying the point positively to the surface for a second and then pulling it away from the edge of the square to the middle, gradually increasing speed and reducing pressure. Repeat all the way down one side. Make sure that you cease to have contact with the surface around halfway through each stroke. 'Flick' strokes of this kind are always much easier if you are pulling the point *towards* you. Repeat on the opposite side of the square.

3A

Set the point until it glows slightly. Start on any edge, and push the point into the surface, holding the pencil so that it is almost vertical. Work around all four edges in this way, and when you have completed a 'circuit', begin another inside the first. You will find it easier to produce even lines if you turn the board at the end of each completed row.

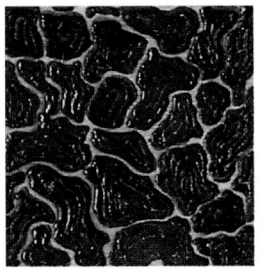

1B

Use a temperature setting similar to that used in 1A, and mark out a series of shapes that are interspaced equally. If you are nervous of doing this with the point, use a soft pencil and then work around each outline with the wire-point to produce bold demarcations. Next, move inwards, burning another line adjacent to the previous, until you have worked your way to the middle of the shape and thus completely filled it. Repeat with all the other shapes until each one becomes a little 'island' of dark texture.

2B

Marks like these are made by working with the grain, with the point making contact with the surface at an angle of 45°. The idea is to use as much of the broad part of the point as possible, to make a wide mark. Begin by marking a series of pencil lines about a millimetre apart, with the grain, as a guide. Set the temperature high enough to give a positive dark line while working slowly and pressing quite hard. Start at the top of the square, pulling the point towards you, but breaking the line at random intervals by lifting the point from the wood. Work your way down the square in this way to create a 'brickwork' effect. Now turn the temperature down considerably and repeat the process, working on the areas previously left out.

3B

This effect is best achieved by using the side of the tip of the point. Use a soft pencil to draw 10–12 wavy lines at random from the top to the bottom of the square. Set the temperature of the point fairly low and aim to produce a fine but positive line. (You may find it helpful to practise on a piece of ply until you get the hang of this.) Start from one side of the square with a row of lines leading from the edge to the first wavy line. Continue along the square with the next set of lines, angled in the opposite direction. Then produce another set of lines at a similar angle to the first. The square shown here was begun on the right-hand side, and all the first lines are about equidistant. As you progress across the square, you can see that the wavy lines cause the gaps to widen in some places, adding interest to the overall texture.

1C

Increase the temperature of the point until it is glowing pink. Start in the middle, making short marks in random directions that touch one another. Work quickly to avoid excessive burning of the wood, and try to ensure consistency between the marks by maintaining an even period of contact for each one. This level of burning will produce some smoke – disperse it as you work by gently blowing it away, but try not to blow on the point of the tool as this will cool it and affect the consistency of the burning. When you get to the edges of the square, turn the heat down a little so that you can slow down and ensure an accurately-burned edge.

2C
Use the point at the setting that makes it glow pink, and practise this texture on a piece of scrap wood before you try it out on your sampler. You need to apply the tip with a modicum of pressure for the shortest possible time. As soon as the point has made contact it must be pulled away from the surface – a 'flick' stroke, rather like producing a comma when you write with a Biro. Repeat this type of mark until you fill the square.

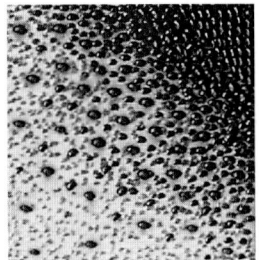

3C
Set the tool to a fairly high temperature, so that the tip glows very slightly, and then turn it down until there is no visible glow.
These dots were all made with the tool at the same setting, but using different periods of contact with the wood. Start at the top right-hand corner, producing dots slowly, using little pressure. As you move towards the opposite side of the square, spread the dots out. Repeat this process, this time reducing the time the point is in contact with the wood, thereby reducing the density of the dot. Then repeat again, this time just touching the surface for a moment each time.

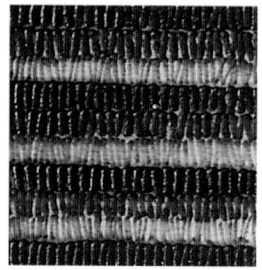

1D

Lightly draw with a soft pencil a series of six equally-spaced lines, going down the square. Use the same temperature as 3C and mark a series of lines slowly in a row, going from left to right between the top of the square and the first pencil line. Use enough pressure and speed to make positive dark lines. Repeat with the row beneath, but speed up enough to produce significantly lighter lines. Repeat again with the third row, even more lightly, and then do another set of three lines graded in the same way, from dark to light.

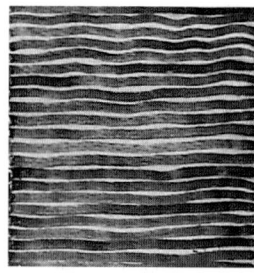

2D

Turn the surface so that you can pull the point towards you with the grain. Set the temperature low enough to make a lightly-burned line. You must be able to exert as much pressure as possible without bending the point of the tool. Use the flat of the point, and draw it towards you, trying to make as deep a groove as possible. Repeat each line as near to the previous one as possible, but don't necessarily create straight lines.

3D

This type of texturing is quite hard to produce, but has many applications, so persevere! Use a low temperature setting, with just enough heat to scorch the wood. Position the end of the point slightly on its side or at an angle, so that only a part of it makes contact with the surface, resulting in a thinner line than those in 2D. Push the point with as much pressure as you can and in as many directions as possible, all over the square. Try to severely mark the surface, rather than burn it. Consistency is the difficulty here: you need to work quickly and continuously so that the heat of the point is absorbed by the surface. Do not stop, even for a moment, as this will cause the point to reheat and, when reapplied, burn the surface more severely than before. It can help to blow gently on the point before contact. Once you have completed the square with a consistent area of tone, start from the top again but work more slowly. The point will fall into the grooves already made, enabling you to create a dark-to-light effect down the square.

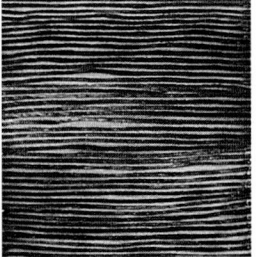

4A

Turn the surface so you can pull the point towards you, with the grain. Set the temperature to an average heat (so that the spoon does not glow). Using the edge of the spoon like a knife, pull it towards you, cutting a line from one side of the square to the other. You will find this quite easy working with the grain – the wood offers little resistance. Repeat the lines one after the other and as near to each other as possible, until the square is filled.

5A

Increase the temperature until there is a slight glow from the spoon point. Hold the pencil in a more vertical position, and push the tip into the surface. Repeat all over the square, leaving a visible gap between each mark. Using a lot of heat in this way produces an overburning effect around each mark, so that, although you are spacing the marks, the surface between each becomes scorched.

6A

This square is produced in a similar way to 5A, but the results are very different, and you will need to take more care and exert more control. Turn the temperature down slightly from the setting used in 5A, which should produce a similar but lighter mark with the tip of the spoon point. Burn a series of marks along the top of the square, angled to the right for the first line, to the left for the second, and so on, until you have filled up the whole square. Take your time and make the marks as similar as possible to one another.

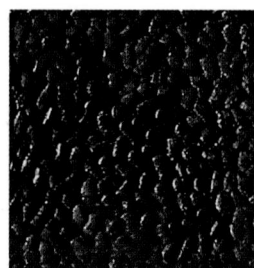

4B

The most important thing with this square is to have the correct temperature setting. The tip needs to be just hot enough to produce a very black mark by pushing the convex side of the spoon point positively into the surface. Begin in the middle of the square and carefully produce each mark so that it just touches the previous mark. Avoid going over the top of a previous mark as this may remove some of the burnt effect. This technique will result in a build-up of carbon on the spoon point, which is easily removed by gently stroking the point's surface on an old piece of sandpaper. Be careful here as too much abrasion will rough up the surface and make it more susceptible to collecting carbon deposits. When you come to work at the edges of the square, turn the temperature down slightly, remembering to increase the time of contact and the pressure to compensate for this.

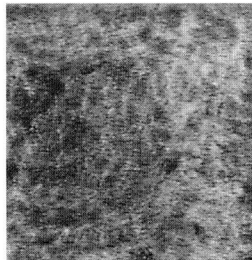

5B

The convex side of the spoon point is used to create this square, with a much lower temperature setting than 4B. Aim to singe the surface in an even manner, without applying too much pressure. Start somewhere in the middle and gently shade the surface in a circular motion, moving on when the required depth of colour is achieved. Take care not to linger on one spot, as this will create uneven burning and ruin the effect. Once again, try to finish the square in one go.

6B

The first stage in creating this effect is exactly the same as that described in 5B, only using a higher temperature, giving you a darker effect. Then, using the edge of the spoon point, cut through the singed surface in a shading motion, starting on one corner. It is easier to cover a small area of approximately 3⁄8in (10mm) at a time. The hot edge removes the singed surface, effectively 'etching' into it. You may need to stop occasionally to remove carbon from the point of the tool.

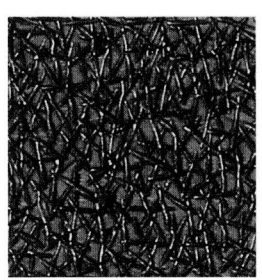

4C

Turn up the temperature until the point is glowing red hot (but no hotter – this damages the point and can cause it to melt). At this temperature you only have to touch the surface to create a positive mark, which will be surrounded by singed wood. Make a series of short marks over the square, with plenty of space around each one. Turn the surface slightly and repeat, so that the next set of marks run in a different direction. Once you have done this two or three times, you won't be able to make further marks without touching previous ones. Continue so that the marks begin to run into one another until the marking of the square is evenly balanced.

5C

Set the point at a temperature to enable you to make a fairly dark mark by working slowly with a lot of pressure. Each mark should be dark at the beginning and tail off to a lighter shade as the heat is absorbed by the wood, and the pressure is reduced. Once you have mastered this technique, make the marks in groups of three or four, starting each subsequent group at 90° from the previous set.

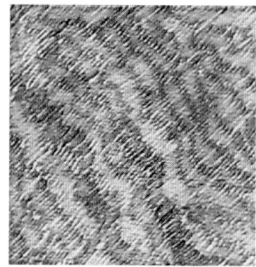

6C

This effect is achieved by repeating the second stage of 6B, but at a moderate temperature, so that the point is hot but not actually glowing. Use a shading motion with the edge of the tool, either working in a small area at a time or, as I did, from the top left-hand corner down to the bottom-right.

4D

Set the temperature reasonably low and, using the edge of the point, cut a short, dark line. Produce a series of groups of lines, identically spaced and at different angles, making sure each group is isolated to start with. Always turn the surface to change direction, not the pyrography pencil. Once you have produced ten or twelve groups of marks, repeat the process, linking up the groups. You can vary the texture considerably, depending on the weight of each group of lines, and the amount of space left between each group.

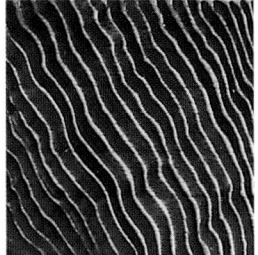

5D

This square requires a low temperature setting combined with pressure and slow, deliberate movements. These are the criteria for accuracy in pyrography. Work diagonally, making sure you are travelling across the grain – take your time and use a low heat, and this should pose no problem. Use the convex side of the spoon point, and pull it towards you across the surface, carefully introducing a slight variation in the direction of the line as you go. Whether you begin in the middle of the square or in one corner, make sure that each line follows the previous one with just a small gap separating them, and take care that the gaps are of an equal width. As you move across the square, try to vary the weight of some of the lines and the pressure used to create them, to produce some interesting variations.

6D

This final square is a variation on 4B. Set the temperature in the same way, but this time work a little faster, using less pressure, producing slightly elongated marks. The result will in fact look like an attempt at 4B where not enough patience was evident!

MAKING A SAMPLER WITH THE SOLID-POINT TOOL

This 24-square sampler shows the great range of tones and textures you can produce with a small selection of solid-points (see Fig 5.4). The references in brackets against each square indicate which solid point was used to create the effect shown. For every square, the temperature was at *full heat*.

	1	2	3	4	5	6
A	B22	P20	P20	22	B22	B24
B	B24	P20	B24	22	B22	B24
C	B24	P20	B22	22	B21	B21
D	B22	B24	B22	22	B21	B21

Fig 5.3 Plan of solid-point sampler.

Fig 5.4 The finished sampler created with the solid-point machine.

1A (B22)

Use the sharp cutting edge of the point, pushing it firmly into the surface. Try to make sure each mark is made using the same amount of pressure and time in contact with the surface. Move the square round after several marks and again after several more, to give marks in different directions, as shown.

1B (B24)

Work fairly rapidly, shading small areas of approximately $\frac{1}{4}$in (6mm) at a time. Shade the areas at random over the square, and then fill in the gaps.

1C (B24)

Work fairly rapidly using the rounded end of the point to fill the whole square without stopping. Use a shading motion, moving the point in as many different directions as you can. Remember that continuous contact with the surface will cool it. If you stop before completing the square, blow on the end of the point just before you restart to avoid a fierce initial burn.

1D (B22)

Use the sharp cutting edge of the point to cut a line from one corner of the square to the other. Twist the edge slightly to form the curves. Repeat from the middle over to one corner, and then do the same to the other corner.

2A (P20)
Use the flat of the point held to the surface for a short time until a very positive black mark is formed. Start towards the middle of the square and work outwards, using the straight side of the point at the edges. This type of intense burning will cause carbon deposits to form on the flat of the point – remove them by gently rubbing the surface over a piece of sandpaper.

2B (P20)
Gently and speedily rub the flat of the point over the surface. Use the minimum of pressure to create an untextured shading effect.

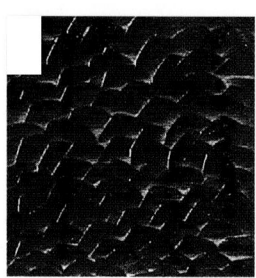

2C (P20)
Use the front end of the flat of the point and push it into the surface to give a deep burn that will fade in intensity as the point is withdrawn from the surface. Repeat the same mark until the whole square is covered.

2D (B24)
Push the point firmly into the surface to produce lines in groups of three. Make about six similar detached groups and then turn the sampler round and pyrograph a second set, making the lines weave out from the first set. Turn the sampler again and repeat until the square is filled.

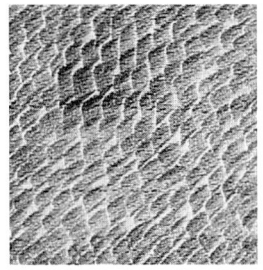

3A (P20)

Use the tip of the point at an angle that prevents the flat coming into contact with the surface. Make *brief* contact, pulling the point towards you. Cont-inue this action and try to make all the marks as similar as possible – ideally by completing the whole square without stopping.

3B (B24)

Push the rounded end of the point vertically into the surface, and repeat until you have filled the square. Try to use the same amount of pressure for each mark, and ensure that all the marks are roughly the same distance apart, producing a uniformly textured area.

3C (B22)

Use the cutting edge of the point and work quickly with moderate pressure to produce groups of five or six short lines, pulling the point towards you. Repeat at equidistant intervals over the square until the total area of lines equals the area of untouched surface. Then turn the sampler 90° and repeat the exercise, filling in all the gaps.

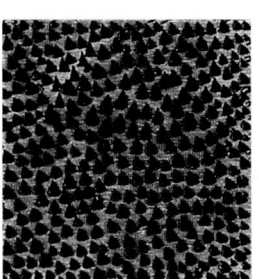

3D (B22)

Push the end of the cutting edge gently into the surface to produce triangular-shaped marks like these, until the whole square is covered.

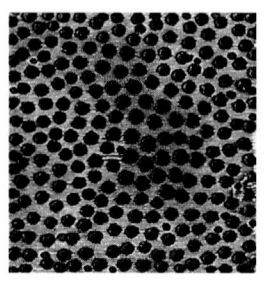

4A (22)
Push the point vertically into the surface. The amount of pressure you use will determine the depth and therefore the size of each mark. Repeat at intervals until the square is covered. The density of this type of toning depends entirely on the amount of space you choose to leave between each mark.

4B (22)
Apply the point at an angle to the surface making the briefest of contacts before flicking it away. Repeat, in as many different directions as possible to produce a square of uniform texture.

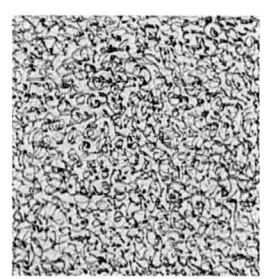

4C (22)
Apply the tip of the point with very little pressure while keeping it moving all the time. Scribble over the surface, changing direction constantly. Try and complete the square in one go.

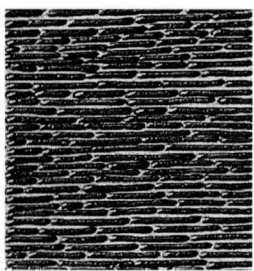

4D (22)
Going with the grain, push the tip of the point into the surface and pull it towards you for a short distance before breaking and continuing. Repeat this, working your way down the square and making sure the breaks occur at different points on each line.

5A (B22)

This time, drag the edge of the point *across* the surface rather than cutting into it. Work your way from left to right, leaving a space between each mark that is equal to the size of the mark. When you reach the bottom of the square, turn the sampler through 90° and repeat the exercise.

5B (B22)

Use approximately half of the point's cutting edge by placing the point at an angle to the surface, and make a row of short cuts across the top of the square. Produce a similar row immediately below the first and so on until the square is completed.

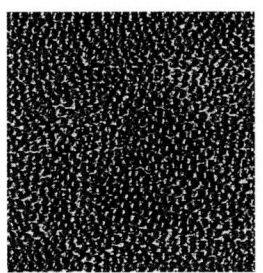

5C (B21)

Push the tip of the point vertically into the surface and keep repeating the same mark. Try to ensure that all the marks are close to each other, if not actually touching.

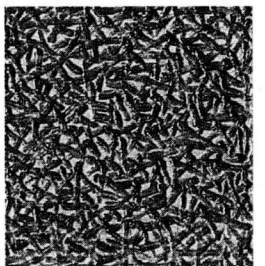

5D (B21)

Apply the point at an angle to the surface and drag it a short distance before removing it from the surface. Repeat until the square is filled, varying direction as often as possible.

6A (B24)

Start in the middle of one side of the square and pos-ition the surface so you can pull the point of the tool towards you, *with* the grain. Give the lines a deliberate wave effect, leaving the odd gap as you progress across the square. The density of the effect is deter-mined by the gaps you leave between the lines.

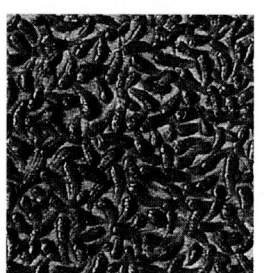

6B (B24)

Apply the point at an angle to the surface. Make positive but brief contact, before flicking away. Repeat in as many directions as possible to produce a uniform square.

6C (B21)

Use as much pressure as possible and work quickly to build up a series of identical, touching lines. Work in the direction of the grain and position the surface so that you can pull the point towards you.

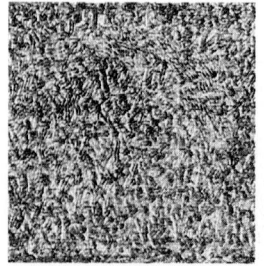

6D (B21)

Even at a high temperature it is difficult to burn a very dark line with this type of point. Use plenty of pressure and pyrograph speedily using a scribbling motion. Try to produce a texture on the surface that results from the pressure you are applying rather than on the heat of the point burning the wood.

6
A SIMPLE COMPOSITION

This exercise shows how you can apply what you have learned so far to a simple piece of work, and at the same time gets to grips with the problem that torments so many beginners: how to produce a constant and continuous line.

Begin by picking a varied selection of interesting-looking grasses from the garden or the roadside, and attach a row of them to a large piece of card or ply using masking tape (see Fig 6.1).

Fig 6.1 A collection of grasses taped to a piece of ply.

Prepare a piece of birch-faced plywood about 5 x 7in (127 x 178mm) (see page 21). The ideal surface for this type of composition will have the grain running lengthways rather than from side to side.

ENGRAVING THE STEMS

With the wood placed so that the grain runs vertically, engrave five or six lines near the bottom to represent the grass stems. Make sure some of the lines reach a point approximately two thirds of the way up the wood. Use a little artistic licence and allow the lines to 'wave in the wind' – see Fig 6.2. You will soon realize that this apparently simple task is actually quite difficult. There are several approaches to engraving straight lines, and it is best that you choose the one from the following list that you find easiest:

▌ Use the side of the wire, an average-to-low temperature setting and a fair amount of pressure. Either push the wire along the wood or turn the wood around and pull the point slowly towards you.

▌ Make a groove in the surface by engraving quickly with pressure to create a line that is only lightly burnt. Then use this

Fig 6.2 Engraving the lines.

groove as a guide and follow its course more slowly to produce the desired effect.

▌ Long lines can be produced in sections of about an inch in length, if you find this easier. As long as each section overlaps neatly with the previous one, the line will appear unbroken.

Producing good lines takes practice. Take your time, don't use too much heat, and maintain an even pressure. The wire or point will burn into the surface at a rate precisely in accordance with the duration of its contact with the wood. Hence, if you falter or jerk as you push or pull the point along the surface, you can expect an uneven and inconsistent line. It's always easier to work *with* the grain. It is possible to pyrograph a line across the grain, but you need to use even less heat, more pressure, and have a very steady hand, as the grain will tend to obstruct the progress of the point.

ENGRAVING THE SEEDS

Choose one of your pieces of grass and study it carefully, taking note of how the seed section at the top is composed. You are not aiming to draw or copy it, but to find a way of *suggesting* the subject by means of pyrography. Refer back to the wide range of tones and textures given in Chapters 4 and 5 and see if you can identify something suitable.

I recommend the texture given for square 2C on page 33, combined with square 4B on page 36. Many wild grass seeds such as wild barley and wheat have seeds which can be represented pyrographically by pushing the point into the wood and drawing it swiftly out and along – a 'flick' stroke (see Fig 6.3). Spend time practising this stroke, as it has numerous applications.

The best pyrographs are those that have a range of light and dark tones, textures and lines. Don't fall into the trap of making all your work a compilation of similarly-weighted lines and marks. Look at

Fig 6.3 Executing a right flick stroke.

the grasses you have collected, and ensure that you create dark areas and marks where they occur, interspersed with lighter and more delicate work (see Fig 6.4). Remember, you are not trying to produce an exact likeness of the subject, but to *suggest* it, so feel free to experiment with your designs as you go along.

ADDING DEPTH

The next stage is to add some depth to the composition. Here are three suggestions:

1   Working from the bottom of the pyrograph, use a B pencil to draw (very lightly) a series of vertical lines to represent blades

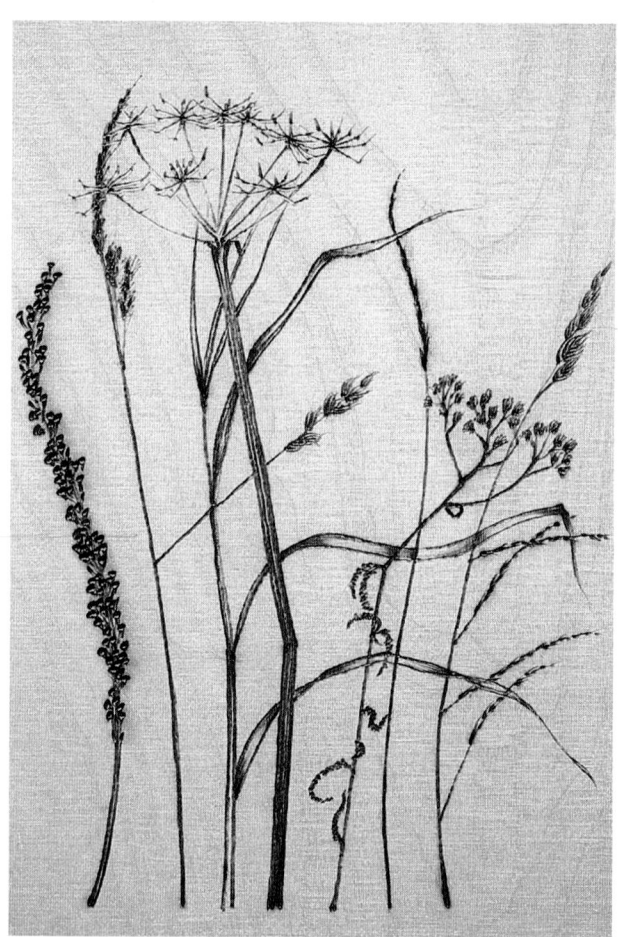

Fig 6.4
The finished
pyrograph.

of grass. Make it interesting by allowing the lines to weave and overlap occasionally. Refer to squares 3C and 3D from the hot-wire sampler (see pages 33 and 34), that dealt with tones changing from dark to light. Pyrograph behind each blade of grass, starting at the bottom and beginning with a very dark tone and gradually fading into a lighter tone (see Fig 6.5). Use a dot texture and either increase your speed as you work up the design or decrease the temperature of the point at intervals from bottom to top. Alternatively, you can use virtually any simple texture, or even a simple pattern, providing the effect is one of a gradual tonal change from dark to light. This background will give the composition some depth, especially if you make the dark areas as black as possible, as shown in the samplers (see Chapter 5).

2 This effect is most easily achieved using a spoon point. Repeat the process described above, but substitute the B pencil lines for pyrographed lines. Where you have an arrangement of blades of grass weaving and overlapping, instead of working on the areas of wood behind the subject, shade in the parts of the subject you would normally expect to be in shadow. Many types of grass, especially when dried, have interesting leaf formations, as if the blades have been twisted into ribbons. These can also be added to your composition using this method, but this time showing the leaves starting from the actual stem.

Fig 6.5 You can add depth by drawing in blades of grass at the base of your illustration and pyrographing dark-fading-gradually-to-light tones behind them.

Fig 6.6 Pyrograph blades of grass at the base, and then shade in the shadow areas using the spoon point.

Try to weave them in and around the other stems and grasses (see Fig 6.6).

3   This is probably the easiest method of adding depth, and is certainly the quickest and least complex. Use the spoon point, and set the temperature to an average-to-low setting. Use the largest surface area of the spoon point and burn a series of slow, deliberate and – as far as possible – black lines from the bottom of the design. Again, make them interesting and realistic by allowing them to wave around a little and weaving in and out of each other. Then burn some fairly lengthy and gradually fading strokes from the base of the design and through the original dark lines (see Fig 6.7).

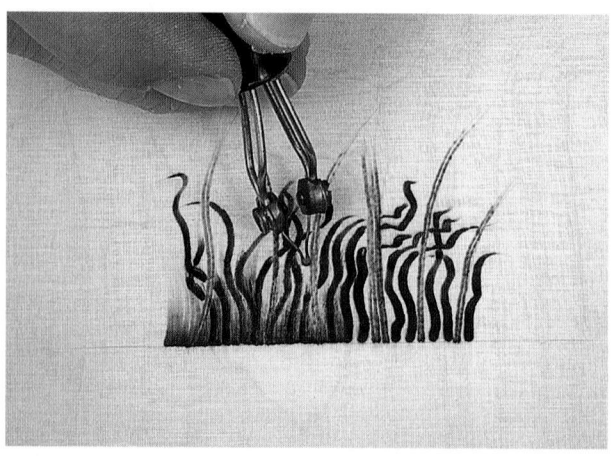

Fig 6.7 Also at the base, interweave some black wavy lines and a few longer, gradually fading, strokes.

7

PRODUCING DEPTH AND TONE

This chapter introduces a tracing technique as a means of transferring a chosen design from its original source to the wood, so that it can be pyrographed. This is a very useful technique, but please read the note on page vi before you begin to copy material for your own use.

You will need:

- A small piece of well-used black pencil carbon paper (a new sheet will suffice if you cannot find a used one).
- A hard pencil (2H), made as sharp as you can get it (use a pencil sharpener and 'fine sharpen' the resulting point with a Stanley knife or scalpel).
- A photocopy of a simple line drawing. Fig 7.1 is ideal – feel free to use it for this exercise.
- Masking tape. *Never* use Sellotape – it will almost certainly lift tiny pieces of the wood surface when you remove it.

First cut the photocopied image out, leaving a small border around it. This gives you an edge to attach it to the wood. You should have enough space in the upper areas of the previous exercise (see Chapter 6) to fit the butterfly in over the grasses. Alternatively, prepare another piece of birch-faced plywood (see page 21).

Decide on the best position for the butterfly and attach the photocopy to the wood with the piece of carbon paper *underneath*. Be very careful not to press the image too hard with your hand or allow your ring or bracelet to press against it, as this will cause an unwanted mark to appear on the wood surface, which is not easy to remove.

Fig 7.1 Butterfly template.

Follow the outline of the top of the butterfly's right-hand wing with the 2H pencil, with one short, precise line (see Fig 7.2). Lift up the master without altering its position and check the line you have just traced. It should be thin and fine – hardly visible in fact. If it is too dark, you have pressed too hard. If it is too broad, then the pencil isn't sharp enough. Pressing too hard can also dent the wood slightly, so gently does it!

Trace the whole butterfly in this way, checking periodically that you are still getting a thin, feint line. Mark in the two dots to represent antennae, but don't put in the actual antennae yet. Check that no detail has been missed by lifting the master up and down rapidly, so that you get a fast comparison of the two images. If you are satisfied, remove the master from the wood.

ANTENNAE

The next stage is to pyrograph the antennae. Lines like these are very difficult to go over a second time, so practise on a scrap of spare wood until you are confident. Set the point temperature fairly low – you are aiming to produce two long flick

Fig 7.2 Transferring the butterfly onto the wood.

strokes, which should not be too dark. Hold the point on the wood where you traced the tip of one of the antennae for a *fraction* of a second, and then pull the line in towards the head. Repeat for the second antenna. Be confident and positive when aiming for effects of this sort, and try to get them right first time.

OUTLINE AND VEIN LINES

Use a similar temperature setting to the antennae. Use a fair amount of pressure, and be sure to burn the

trace lines out completely. Work slowly to ensure accuracy, and remember to have a scrap of wood handy to test the point on.

Begin on the outside of the butterfly's wings, and try to finish each line in one go. Once the outer edges of the wings are complete, add the lines that represent the veins. These need to be pushed quite deeply into the wood, so use the side of the point, which is the strongest and least likely to bend (see Fig 7.3).

Next, carefully burn in the traced lines of the body (thorax), and add two dots for the eyes.

Fig 7.3 Pyrographing the vein lines on the wings.

WINGS

The wings require the use of the spoon point. Try out the effects you need to achieve on scrap wood until you are happy with them. The object is to fill the wings with a tone or texture that corresponds to the soft texture of a real butterfly's wing. Set the temperature of the point so that, with a little pressure, a dark line can be formed, but which still enables you to work slowly and accurately without 'overburning' (see page 26).Work from the outside of the wing towards the body, stopping short of the body itself. Your shading lines should follow the direction of the vein lines, and begin dark, becoming lighter as you move inwards. The natural cooling of the spoon point as you work will be a great aid to achieving this effect (see Fig 7.4). When you get to the end of the outer wing edge, repeat the process carefully in the other direction, working from the body outwards. Don't worry about going over the vein lines; if you pyrographed them deeply enough it will be impossible for the spoon

Fig 7.4 Shading the wings with the spoon point.

Fig 7.5 Flick stroking the hairs on the body.

point to obliterate them. Now repeat
the process with the other wing.
The completed effect should give an
almost three-dimensional
appearance to the butterfly's wings.

BODY

As this butterfly is not intended to
represent any particular species,
there is scope to borrow interesting
features from a number of species.
For example, many butterflies have
quite hairy bodies, such as the small
tortoiseshell. This is a good texture
to try and reproduce, and also a
good example of how pyrography

can sometimes have the edge over
other mediums.

Begin by gently shading in the
body area with the spoon point,
using the same temperature setting
as you did for the wings. Visualize a
line running down the centre of the
body, and, working from this line
outwards, make some flick strokes
with the edge of the spoon point to
represent hairs (see Fig 7.5). The
sharp edge of the spoon point will
cut into the wood surface, and
where it is applied over existing
burnt areas, will cut through them.
This is why this effect has to be
applied last.

8
PRODUCING LIFELIKE TEXTURES

The projects in this chapter are designed to further develop your skills in the pyrographic reproduction of tones and textures found in nature. In the course of producing two designs (a mouse and a blackberry), you will learn how to realistically represent the look and texture of natural features such as fur, skin, eyes, leaves, berries, stalks and stems.

MOUSE

First take a photocopy of the mouse template shown in Fig 8.1. You will see that there are no actual lines to trace other than those that represent the ears, eyes and paws. The dots are directional guide marks to show you where the pyrographed lines will begin and which direction they travel. The exercise has a dual purpose: first, it will show you how to make a pyrograph almost entirely by the use of texture, and second it will show you how any illustration or photograph (especially wildlife subjects) can be transferred in the form of a plan onto a wood surface.

The design (Fig 8.1) represents the maximum number of lines and marks you would need when tracing from an original picture or a photocopy. Remember – the lines and marks are guides for you to follow with the pyrography pencil, and will eventually be burnt away. Hence, the more marks there are, the harder it becomes to eradicate them – so, keep it simple. Once you have traced the marks onto the wood (see Fig 8.2), you can concentrate on the detail by referring to the original picture, secure in the knowledge that you have the proportions of the subject correct.

Fig 8.1 Mouse template.

Fig 8.2 The mouse transferred to the wood.

TRACING

Trace the details of the mouse template onto the wood as with the butterfly exercise (see page 53). Ensure you trace *precisely* what is there, and that where the marks are directional, yours are the same. Take care to press gently, making very light marks with the carbon. The outline of the eyes is very important; as is usual with a life subject or portrait, the viewer's eyes will focus on the eyes of the subject, so if they are wrong it will be the first thing that is noticed. When you are satisfied that the template has been fully traced, remove it and attach it further up the wood so that you can refer to it easily.

If some areas of the carbon are darker than others, you can sand them down gently using very worn sandpaper (if you can't find any, rub two pieces of new sandpaper together to wear them down). Don't use a pencil rubber, as this is likely to cause smudging. If the sandpaper removes some of the fine detail, restore it with a pencil, using the template as a guide.

EYES

Work on the eyes first – this will help you to visualize the finished design much easier from the start. Set the point to a very low temperature – even though you are aiming to create a dark area, you will need to work slowly to maintain accuracy. Carefully pyrograph the outline of the eyes first, and then work inwards, burning as dark as you can, leaving a tiny area within each eye to represent the highlight (see Fig 8.3).

Now begin on the fur. It doesn't matter how light the pyrographed lines are, because once the grooves are in the wood they can easily be darkened by going over them again, either more slowly or using a higher temperature setting. However, if you make the lines too dark to begin with, you are stuck with them!

Use a low temperature setting to pyrograph a series of short, slightly curved flick strokes around the left eye (see Fig 8.4). Make sure each mark starts a little bit away from the eye, and that the flick stroke is what the word suggests, not a short line. Study Fig 8.4 carefully, to make sure the direction of your marks is correct. The two different textures of the eye and the surrounding fur will give the impression that the eye is in a socket and not just 'stuck on'.

Before working on the other eye, you need to do some work around it. You will see a row of marks running from the top of the right eye to the base of the ear. Working in an outward direction, flick stroke these in, and then do the same with the marks that appear down the side of the face, only this time work inwards (see Fig 8.5). *All* the marks representing fur lines need to be pyrographed inwards to prevent the formation of double lines. Finally, pyrograph the marks that represent the mouse's face.

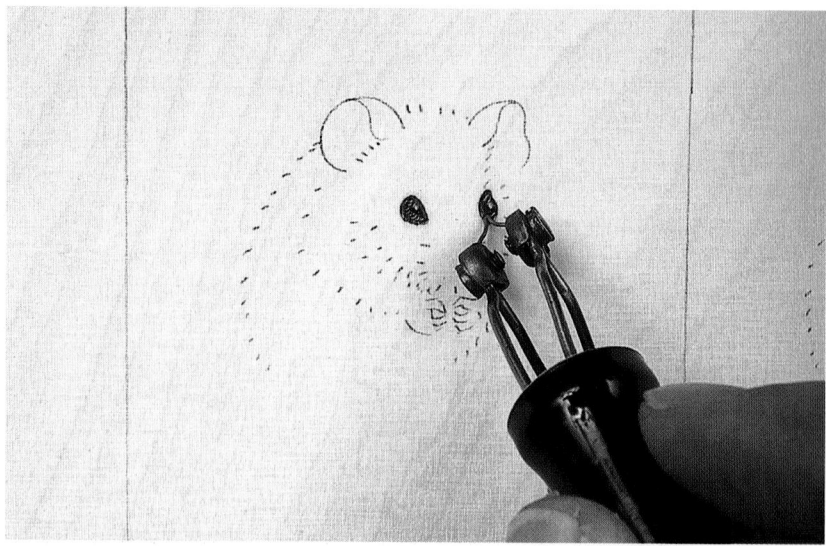

Fig 8.3 Burning in the eyes.

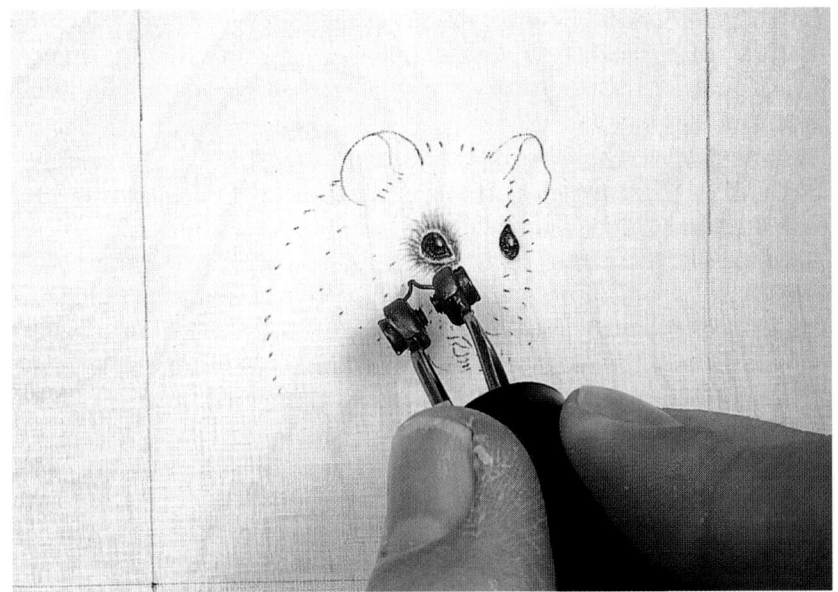

Fig 8.4 Short flick strokes are inserted around the left eye to suggest the eye is slightly recessed within the head.

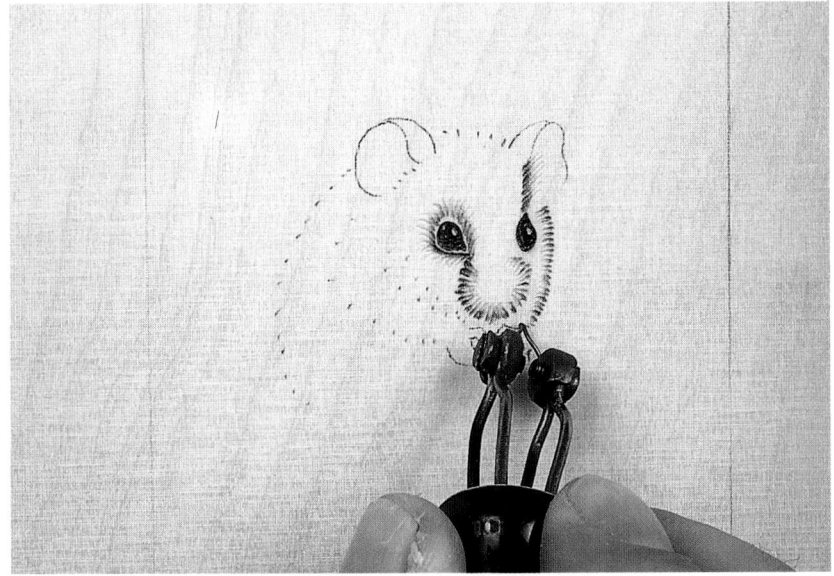

Fig 8.5 Flick stroking the fur marks delineating the edge of the mouse's face.

Now texture the right eye. Again, working from a point just short of the actual eye, pyrograph a series of short lines using a little more pressure, working from the eyeball outwards, as with the left eye. These lines and this texture will form the side of the face (see Fig 8.6).

OUTLINE

Working from the outside, pyrograph all the remaining trace marks in a similar manner to the previous ones (see Fig 8.7). Keep religiously to the direction of the marks, and fill in the gaps between each mark with additional marks. It doesn't matter how many extra little marks you pyrograph; what is important is that you keep them in a neat line around the body of the mouse, so that its fur doesn't appear ruffled, and so that the carbon trace lines are burnt away.

TEXTURE

Start at the top of the mouse's head and pyrograph slightly longer lines (effectively, long flick strokes) in the direction shown in Fig 8.8. Make sure these lines don't have ends or blobs. Continue with this texture, working your way to the bottom of the mouse's face, and then work the

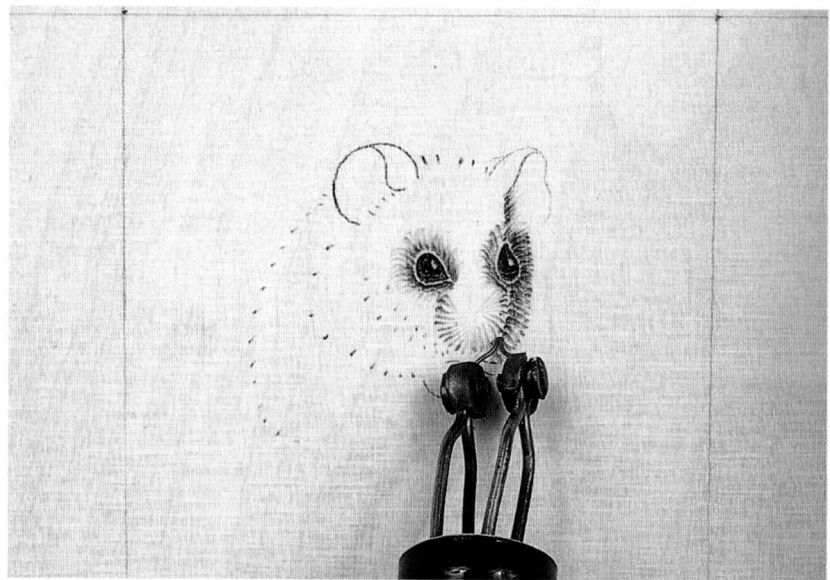

Fig 8.6 With the right eye complete, further work is done on developing the texture on the side of the face.

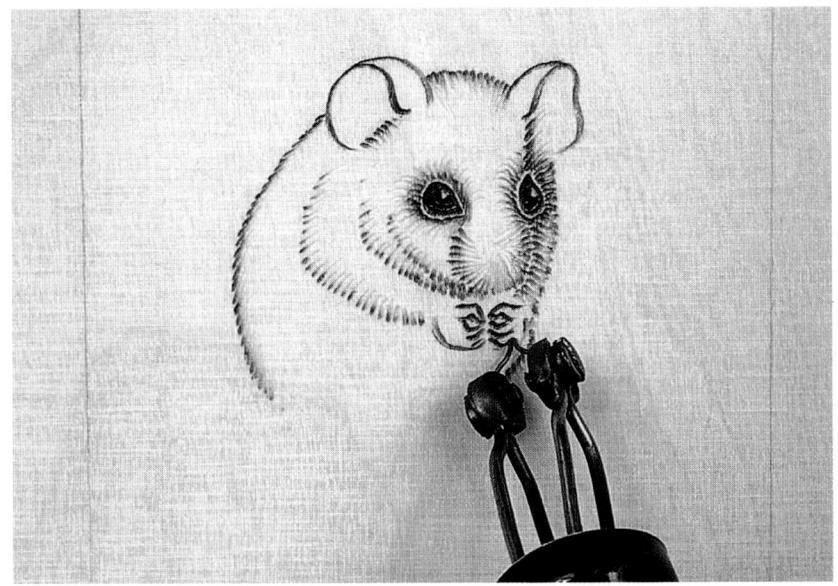

Fig 8.7 Pyrographing the remaining trace marks.

Fig 8.8 Putting in the texture of the mouse's fur.

lines from there up to the left ear. The lines should appear to 'funnel' down between the eyes. Again, it is the *texture* that is important; don't worry if the lines are too light at this stage.

The next stage utilizes the double-line effect that up to now you have been trying to avoid. Link up the marks that represent the left cheek with the marks you made around the left eye, using a curved line to emphasize the roundness of the face. Repeat this process, using a touch more heat, linking the marks that represent the top of the forearm with the eye area. You

should get a subtle double-line effect, which assists in the three-dimensionality of the image (see Fig 8.8). Repeat the process for a third time from the bottom of the arm to meet the texture at the bottom of the eye.

Although your mouse may not be very dark at this stage, if you shine your work lamp across it you should see a definite furry texture. To complete this stage, treat the mouse's back as shown in Fig 8.8, maintaining a slight curve to each pyrographed line and increasing the arc as you get nearer to the part below the paws.

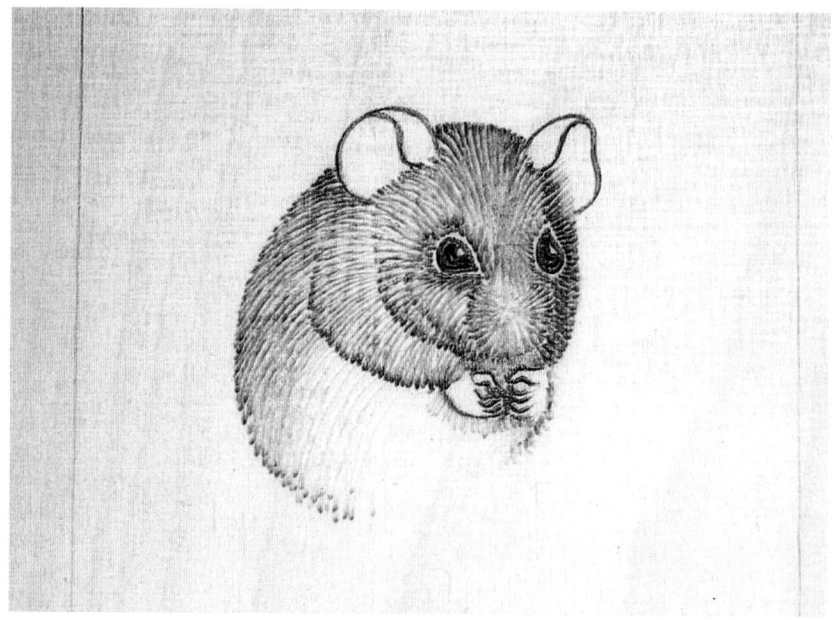

Fig 8.9 The fur lines are darkened to enhance the overall look and texture of the mouse.

To increase the three-dimensional effect of the multi-grooved texture, you need to work further on some parts of the mouse so as to darken them (see Fig 8.9). Use a slightly higher temperature and work slowly over the following areas:

▌ From the top of the head, down through the front of the face.
▌ The right-hand side of the face.
▌ The back, from a point starting behind the left ear.
▌ Behind the paws.

EARS AND WHISKERS

Finally, you need to add some texture to the ears, and pyrograph in the whiskers. The outer parts of the ears should be carefully shaded in with the point. Use very little pressure and a low temperature setting. It is important to differentiate between the furry texture of the body and the soft, skin-like surface of the ears. Make your strokes from the top to the bottom of the area as uniform as you can.

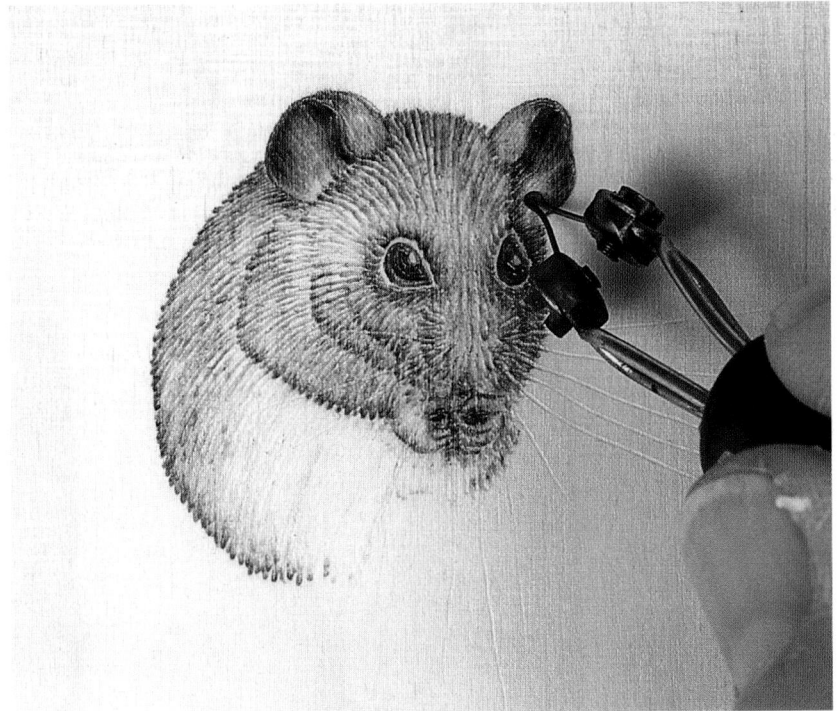

Fig 8.10 Working on the mouse's ears.

Being in shadow, the inner part of the ears must be made much darker, and for this you will need the spoon point. The idea is to produce a small, dark area without pressing too hard and thereby creating unwanted texture, so work very slowly with a low temperature setting. As you get towards the outer edge of the ear, gradually decrease the pressure and slightly increase your speed. This will create a graduated paling of the dark, shaded area, and will help to suggest depth (see Fig 8.10).

Now give your mouse some whiskers. Use a point at the lowest possible setting and, working from the face outwards, make a few rapid cuts outwards. The effect of the whiskers is caused by the minute shadow created by light passing across the cut marks, rather than by any actual burning of the wood.

Fig 8.11 Blackberry panel template.

BLACKBERRIES

This design was pyrographed on a plaque of kiln-dried sycamore measuring $\frac{9}{16}$ x 7 x 10in (14 x 178 x 254mm), which was supplied by Janik.

TRACING THE DESIGN

Photocopy Fig 8.11 to the size you require. Cut down the photocopy to a size slightly less than the wood surface, and position and attach it with masking tape. Carefully trace through using carbon paper in the usual way (see Fig 8.12). Don't spend too much time on minute detail at this stage (such as the thorns) – just mark their positions.

Once you are satisfied with the tracing, remove the plan and tidy up any areas that are too bold, either with a pencil rubber (being very careful not to smudge the lines) or with sandpaper. Fill in any missed areas lightly with a 2B pencil.

Fig 8.12
The completed
tracing.

OUTLINE

Use the wire point to burn away the traced outline (see Fig 8.13). You can make the edges of the leaves more realistic at this stage by defining them more accurately. Set the wire point to an average temperature to allow you to engrave at a reasonable speed without overburning or singeing the wood around the trace lines. Use your piece of scrap wood to test you have

the right temperature before beginning. You will find it helpful to turn the wood as you work.

Next, use a slightly lower temperature to burn in the thorn outlines: two short curved flick strokes from the stem that meet to form a sharp point. Push fairly hard at the beginning to ensure the thorn has a fat base. The size of each thorn is dictated by the amount of pressure you apply, and the speed at which you work.

Fig 8.13 The outline, including the thorns, partially pyrographed.

BERRIES

Once all the traces of carbon have been removed by the pyrography, you can start on the berries. Turn the temperature down still further – you will be working very slowly with lots of pressure to obtain the blackest marks possible. Use the rounded end of the point rather than angling it to the surface; this will minimize the forming of any unwanted texture on what is essentially a smooth subject. Be patient, work slowly, and you will achieve a *very* black result. The berry segments can be treated in an identical way to the eyes of the mouse (see page 59). Leave a small space for a highlight on each berry, making sure it appears in the same area of each segment, and burn in a circular movement, slowly, with a low temperature setting and a reasonable amount of pressure (see Fig 8.14).

Fig 8.14 Some berry segments.

STALKS, STEMS AND LEAVES

Next, fill in the stalks and stems. The stems of a blackberry have a rather rough, woody texture, and you need to try and represent this. To do so you will need a slightly higher temperature, combined with more speed and as much pressure on the *side* of the point as you can manage (see Fig 8.15).

In contrast to the stems, the small leaves at the base of the blackberry have a soft texture similar to the mouse's ear (see page 65). These areas should be shaded using the wire point at a fairly low temperature, using very little pressure. Work from the base of the berry on each of these tiny areas using uniform strokes. This will produce a darker shading effect just where you want it, representing the natural shadow caused by the leaf coming from under the berry (see Fig 8.16).

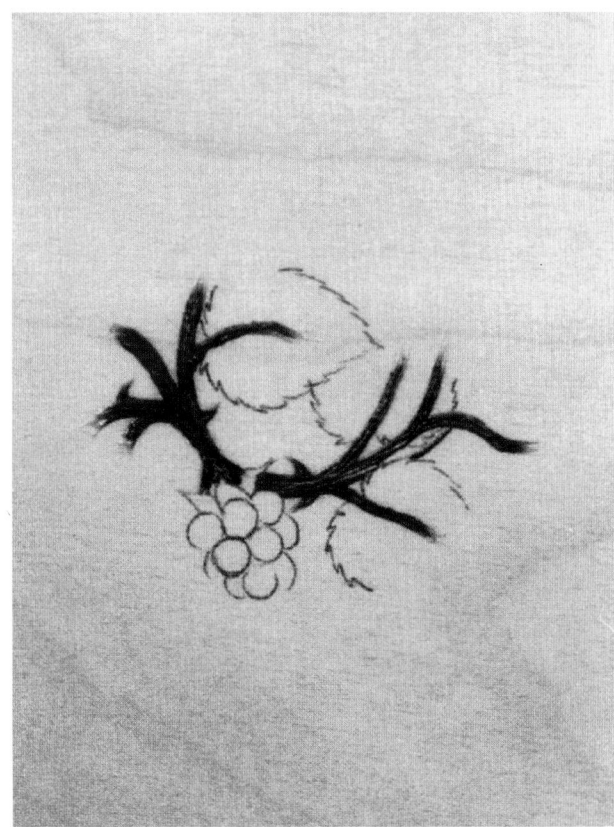

Fig 8.15 Aim for a rough, woody texture for the stalks and stems.

The final stages need a lot of care. Use the spoon point and ensure the temperature setting is exactly right before proceeding. Work from the base of the leaf and from the line you engraved through the centre, using the same technique employed when you produced the dark areas inside the ear of the mouse (see page 66). Work quite slowly at an average heat setting, using as much pressure as you can without actually bending the spoon point. As each broad line is pyrographed deeply into the wood surface, a raised edge will form between each line, suggesting veins and leaves. Remember that the leaves will not all have the same density of colour; some will be tucked behind in shadow and will be quite dark. Trace one or two leaves from your photocopy onto the test wood and practise before working on the actual piece. Always work from the centre of the leaf outwards. The darker area that is formed at the beginning of each mark will add some dimension to the leaf (see Fig 8.17).

Fig 8.16 The small leaves at the base of the berries should have a soft texture.

FINAL TOUCHES

Once all the leaves have been pyrographed, study your work to make sure nothing has been missed out. With a fairly complicated design like this it is easy to miss a small section of stem, or perhaps a thorn. Consider increasing some of the shading with the spoon point where leaves overlap and would create very positive shadows. You may find an extra thorn or two will help to balance a slightly weak or open section of the design.

Finally, decide how to finish the pyrograph: with varnish or polish (see Chapter 13).

Fig 8.17 Some leaves partially completed, showing the dimensional effect obtained by the darker area at the start of each line of shading, and by the placing of some of the leaves in shadow.

Fig 8.18 The completed blackberry panel.

9

SHADING TECHNIQUES

The project in this chapter is a hinge design, chosen as a means of demonstrating how a quite ordinary design can be enhanced by the introduction of shadows and graduated shading, using both wire and spoon points. The resulting design can be used to decorate a box lid or a simpler version could provide a decoration for a small picture frame or used as a repeat pattern for a border.

The flower in the centre of the design (see Fig 9.1) came from a section in a pre-war craft book dealing with the manufacture of paper flowers. The designs on either side of the flower have been adapted from a drawing suggesting a design for an elaborate metal hinge. I simply re-drew the hinge, leaving out the screw fittings and slightly exaggerating the overlapping parts of the design. By tracing my finished line drawing and then reversing it, I produced the mirror image for the other side of the flower.

I suggest you enlarge the design to about 10in (254mm) in length, as the smaller it is the harder it will be to pyrograph, and less detail is possible. I used a standard Janik sycamore plaque of 12 ¾ x 8 ¾in (324 x 222mm), but as always try the design on a piece of birch-faced plywood to begin with until you are confident.

PYROGRAPHING THE LINES

Trace your design through the carbon paper in the usual way. Don't worry too much about producing a dark tracing this time; the lines you need to burn out will be fairly thick. Take care to keep these initial burnings uniform. Set the point to a temperature that allows you to produce a black line slowly and with some pressure. If the point is too hot you will either have to work quickly, or run the risk of overburning (see pages 23–26). Aim to produce a crisp, solid dark line. Remember to avoid working entirely from one side of the design to the other. Complete a section on one side and then complete the equivalent section on the other side. This way, symmetry and continuity will be maintained (see Fig 9.1). Be very careful not to burn a line in the wrong place. With a relatively complex design like this, where there are a host of lines over- and underlapping, a line burned deeply in the wrong place can cause big problems. If you do make an error like this, gently scrape away the mistake with the point of a 10A scalpel blade, and then carefully sand the affected area with a small piece of sandpaper.

Fig 9.1 Hinge template.

Assuming all goes well, you should now have a nicely engraved line drawing of the original design (see Fig 9.2).

SHADING

Use the spoon point for the shading. The correct temperature setting is crucial for the first stage, so spend some time getting it right. Set the temperature very low, so that the spoon has to rest on the wood for a second or two before any mark is made. Then increase the temperature fractionally, and this should be the level of heat you need.

Use minimal pressure, and work slowly and carefully with a stroking movement, shading in the points of the design (see Fig 9.4). Begin with the points within the outer designs, gradually reducing the pressure at the end of each stroke. Try to create the effect of a graduated tint running from dark to light. Once again, work on an area on one side, and then repeat the work on an equivalent area on the other side, and so on, back and forth. Once these points have been shaded, use the same process to shade the points of the flower petals in the centre of the design (see Fig 9.5).

Next, heat the spoon point so that it is red hot, by turning the control dial up *slowly*, and watching the point until it has a slight glow.

Fig 9.2 Pyrographing the lines. Aim for a crisp, solid, dark line, swapping sides as you go, rather than progressing from one side to the other.

Fig 9.3 The lines fully engraved.

Fig 9.4 The points of the design shaded in.

Fig 9.5 The points of the flower shaded in.

Use this temperature to mark in the lines that run from the centre of the flower. After a few practice runs, push the end of the spoon point into the wood on the design, and draw it away from the starting point in a fairly swift cutting movement. If the heat is right, you should hear the tool burning the surface. Here you are aiming to *achieve* over-burning (see Fig 9.6).

Now go back to the hinge part of the design and study it carefully. Then work from the left-hand side and use the spoon point to carefully shade all the little areas that appear to be emerging from beneath other areas. The flower should receive similar treatment, and in order to draw attention to it I have deliberately over-darkened the petals at the back (see Fig 9.7).

FLOWER CENTRE

This is a job for the wire point. The whole area of the flower's centre is made up of tiny C-shaped marks (see Fig 9.8). To create these, set the temperature slightly lower than that used to produce the original outline. Mark in a series of C-shaped marks two lines deep around the outer edge, gradually reducing the pressure as you work towards the middle. Create one more heavily burned C-shape in the centre, and the job is done.

Fig 9.6 The lines on the petals of the flower are achieved by overburning with the spoon point.

Fig 9.7 The shadows on the hinge and the flower are shaded in.

Fig 9.8 A close-up of the flower showing the C-shaped marks that make up its centre burned in.

The design can now be further enhanced by using the wire point, set at the temperature you used at the start for the outline, to create a series of dots, working from the darker shaded areas inwards (see Fig 9.9). As you move towards the otherwise untouched parts of each segment, reduce the pressure and increase your working speed until you are working too fast for the point to actually burn the wood. You need to have the pencil almost upright at this stage to ensure that you are using the tip of the point only. This is a tedious stage, but it is an effective shading method to add to your growing repertoire.

Fig 9.9 The completed design, including the graduated dot effect on the hinge area.

10
ADDING COLOUR

Adding colour to a pyrograph is not a new idea, but unfortunately, many pieces are no more than a burnt outline that has simply been coloured in. Personally, I feel that colour should never take over the pyrograph. It is better to aim for a pyrograph that has been *enhanced* by the careful use of colour than to produce a painting with some pyrography as part of it!

METHODS OF COLOURING

GOUACHE

When applying colour to a pyrograph, the first concern is for the textures already produced on the wood surface, which must be retained, not obscured by solid areas of pigment. In order to preserve the look of the pyrograph, it is best to use a water-soluble paint, and I recommend gouache. This has a stronger, denser pigment than watercolour, but can be diluted with water to the thinnest of applications without losing its colour strength, as watercolours tend to do.

As already stated, the idea is not to obscure skilfully produced textures, but to enhance them. For example, it would be undesirable for the wing of a butterfly, carefully pyrographed to create the effect of the veins, to be covered with a thick coat of colour. Use colour sparingly with plenty of water to thin it when you are mixing; you can build the colour up to the required density gradually, with additional coats. Heavily pyrographed areas of wood, particularly where the spoon point has been used, will not readily accept paint, so the best areas to consider colouring are those that have been lightly pyrographed. They will be more paint receptive without the problem of the paint having nothing to key into.

DYES

Wood dye is available in a variety of colours, but be careful. The dyes are absorbed by the wood much faster than water-based paints, because they are generally spirit or solvent based, designed to soak into the material being dyed, whereas watercolours allow the pigment to sit on the surface, while the water is absorbed. Dyes can be used to good effect, but sparingly, preferably being applied with a small sable brush. (The best way to do this is to

Fig 10.1 A feathery texture was pyrographed before adding colour to this kingfisher in order to produce a more lifelike effect.

Fig 10.2 My version of an eighteenth-century engraving of Newmarket races. In this piece, pyrographed on a solid sycamore block, only one dye was used to vary the densities and achieve the desired effect.

load the brush and then paint with it on a spare piece of wood similar to the one you will be working on, until it ceases to streak out of control.) You will be surprised at how little dye you need and, as with paint, the density of colour can be increased with additional coats. As an extra safeguard, ensure that as many of the areas to be dyed are enclosed and protected by positively engraved lines or solid areas. This will impede the running of the dye.

An example of this use of dye is shown in Fig 10.2. Where you are adding colour to an area that is a combination of heavily pyrographed

marks, and heavily pyrographed marks with little or no heat – for example, the mouse in Chapter 8 – you will need to use a stronger, more concentrated colour, the density of which will be reduced on contact with the combination of minute areas that are non-receptive to the paint, and the minute areas of bare, unpyrographed wood.

The final impression of colour is composed of a range of things: the dark and light of the pyrography, the colour of the bare wood, and the colour of the paint you have added. The texture, undiminished by the addition of colour, will still give the impression of an extra dimension, unachievable by simply adding paint to paper or wood.

COLOURING PROJECT: THREE BUTTERFLIES

This project is a simple introduction to colouring a pyrograph, and also shows by stages how three similar designs treated in different ways will give contrasting results. You will need a piece of sycamore 7 x 10in (178 x 254mm) or similar. Photocopy and enlarge Fig 10.3 so that the butterflies are approximately 2in (51mm) across, and trace this onto the wood using the method described in Chapter 8. With the butterfly on the right, use a pencil rubber after tracing to remove as much of the carbon as possible.

BURNING AWAY THE CARBON OUTLINES

Begin by burning the outlines away (see Fig 10.4). Start with the butterfly in the centre, using a reasonable amount of pressure, and working slowly to produce dark, solid lines.

Use a little less heat and pressure for the butterfly on the left, while still aiming for fairly deep marks in the wood to make the veins in the wings more realistic.

The butterfly on the right will have colour added to it, so dark lines are less important, but *deep* lines are vital. Use a very low temperature setting and exert maximum pressure, using the side of the wire point.

Fig 10.3 Three-butterflies template.

Fig 10.4 The outlines pyrographed.

BUTTERFLY ONE

The idea is to produce a dark, solid butterfly in the centre. Use the spoon point to produce a dark stroke that gradually becomes lighter towards the centre of the butterfly (see Fig 10.5). Don't have the temperature too high – just high enough to give a dark burn without the need for too much pressure. There is a slight danger of overburning here, so you may need to gently blow on the spoon just before making contact with the wood.

Work around the outer edge in this way and then do the same on the inside edge, starting each mark from the outer edge of the body. Here there is a smaller area to cover, so reduce the temperature a little to allow for the shorter strokes you will be making.

To complete the body, shade in the abdomen with the spoon point, slowing down the strokes slightly beneath the stripes to enhance the shading effect. The final touch is to suggest the fine hairs normally seen on this type of insect. At an even lower temperature, use the edge of the spoon and work quickly, to produce a series of cuts from the line in the centre outwards (see Fig 10.6). Practise this effect first; it is very easy to ruin the work at this stage by being overeager.

Fig 10.5 Butterfly One's wings shaded at the outer edge.

Fig 10.6 The inner parts of the wings shaded, and the body pyrographed.

BUTTERFLY TWO

Now work on the left-hand butterfly, beginning by repeating the shading technique used for Butterfly One, but at a much lower temperature and using less pressure. You will find that the spoon glides over the deep lines of the veins in the wings, making them stand out. To test that you have achieved the right result, lay a piece of greaseproof paper over the butterfly and pencil over it with a soft lead. The detail of the deeply pyrographed lines should be clearly visible (see Fig 10.7). Complete the body as described for Butterfly One.

Like the butterfly in Chapter 7 you can choose either a real or imaginary wing pattern for these butterflies, or simply copy mine, shown in Fig 10.8. Begin by marking a few guide lines with a soft pencil, ensuring that the wing designs are symmetrical. When you have a reasonable selection of lines, burn them in with the wire point, and then remove any unused lines with a rubber. Remember not to use too high a temperature or go too fast. Aim for dark, positive lines, tapering (or fading) a little at the ends.

Now change back to the spoon. Work from the line towards the

Fig 10.7 Butterfly Two's wings and body shaded.

Fig 10.8 The markings burned onto the wings with the wire point.

middle of the butterfly, using a low temperature, and gently shade in the area with a stroking movement. Practise this on a piece of scrap wood first. It is a technique well worth mastering, as it produces a quite stunning effect (see Fig 10.9).

BUTTERFLY THREE

The last butterfly is coloured using designer's gouache. Go for a light colour such as white (permanent) or, as I chose, yellow. Use a small sable brush (a no. 1 is ideal for colouring work of this size), dilute the paint slightly with some water, and carefully colour in the wings. As long as the pyrographed lines are

deep (which they should be), and the gouache is not too diluted, the paint will be contained within the desired area. The paint won't readily adhere to the vein lines, so you need to be patient and persevere. Allow the paint to dry (this takes about five minutes) and then apply a second coat. Continue in this way so as to build up a fairly thick coating (see Fig 10.10).

Now choose a darker colour to complement the original colour, and carefully apply a thick line of it on the upper and lower left-hand wings, as shown in Fig 10.11. Try to work from the very edge, and ensure that none of the first colour is showing.

Fig 10.9 Further shading work carried out on the markings, this time with the spoon point.

Fig 10.10 The wings of Butterfly Three coloured with yellow designer's gouache slightly diluted with water.

Now clean your brush thoroughly. To achieve the effect shown in Fig 10.11 you need to gently work the darker colour into the lighter. The brush only needs to be damp, not wet, and the process must be carried out carefully and slowly. Too much moisture or pressure and you will end up removing too much of the under-coat. Repeat the process on the other two, and then complete the body of the butterfly as described on page 90 and shown in Fig 10.12.

You can experiment further with this technique by adding a few more dark lines, and painting some additional patterns on the butterfly using the second colour (see Fig 10.13), along the lines of the pyrography patterns made on Butterfly Two.

Of course, you can also tackle this project using wood dyes instead of paint, and experiment with gentle washes and tints of gouache to colour the background wood surface before pyrography begins.

COLOURING PROJECT: COCKEREL

In this project, pyrography is used to create textures that will enhance the detail of the design, and give a hint of a third dimension.

Fig 10.11 The application of a complementary dark green colour as a thick line at the edge of the upper and lower wings; the right-hand wings show the effect to aim for when working the green into the yellow 'undercoat'.

Fig 10.12 The body of Butterfly Three pyrographed.

Fig 10.13 Optional extra patterns can be applied to the wings of Butterfly Three.

Fig 10.14 Cockerel template.

PYROGRAPHING THE OUTLINE

The template should first be laid down onto the wood in the usual way (see Figs 10.14 and 10.15). I suggest you enlarge the cockerel so that it is about 8in (203mm) high, and use a suitably-sized piece of birch-faced plywood. Sand the wood so that the surface is very smooth, as this will assist with the painting of fine detail. Set the wire point so that it is hot enough to produce a clear burn working at a slow speed, applying as much pressure as you can, to engrave deep lines (see Fig 10.16).

Fig 10.15 The plan of the cockerel transferred to the ply.

TEXTURING

Once you have pyrographed all the outlines, begin the texturing with the wing and tail feathers. Make positive marks that are strong enough to show through the paint. The breast of the bird does not have very much variation of tone, but you will notice a series of V-shaped marks on the design in this area (see Fig 10.16). Use the wire point to

Fig 10.16 The lines of the plan should be pyrographed as deeply as possible. Note the V-shaped marks on the bird's chest.

push some fairly deep gouges over the Vs, working from the bottom up (see Fig 10.17).

You now need to pyrograph the comb and the tiny area of the head where the feathers appear from behind the comb. Real combs are rather pitted flaps of loose skin, and this is the effect you are aiming to produce, by pushing the wire point into the wood of the comb to make a series of dots. Then, using the

Fig 10.17 The wire point is used to texture the chest area, the little white tuft at the base of the tail feathers, and the rear of the bird beneath the wing feathers.

edge of the end of the point, cut in some fine shadow lines and texture lines to represent the fine feathers coming from behind the comb.

Now change to the spoon point, which is the best tool for creating deep pyrographed lines that are to be painted. Use the cutting edge of the spoon at a temperature high enough to aid the point into the wood, and pyrograph a series of deeply-cut lines to represent the

texture of the feathers. This effect is best seen on the larger main tail feathers (see Fig 10.18). The pyrography is now complete apart from the head and feet, which are done at a later stage.

PAINTING

Despite the density of pigment in gouache, it is wise to prepare the work with an undercoat, especially

Fig 10.18 The spoon point is used to create the texture of the main tail feathers and the lower wing feathers in a series of deeply-cut lines.

where the lighter colours are involved. For this reason, apply a coat of permanent white to the areas shown in Fig 10.19. This also ensures that when the other colours are applied to the white you will get a more solid cover than if the colours were applied directly to the wood.

Now you can begin to paint in the large areas of colour. Be a little mean with the amount of paint, so that the engraved lines are not filled

Fig 10.19 A coat of permanent white paint is applied to the areas where lighter colours are to appear.

in. The painting should begin on the head (see Fig 10.20). The white and red on the comb will be fused together using a slightly damp brush to form the required colour. This technique works particularly well with gouache on wood. Paint the neck next. The deep lines you pyrographed to represent the feather formations are your guide to painting in the detail (see Fig 10.21). They will also help to steer

Fig 10.20 The application of colour.

the paint into the areas you want. Finally, pyrograph in the head and feet (see Fig 10.22).

If you want to explore the combination of painting and pyrography further, experiment with other colour mediums, such as coloured dyes. These are less likely to fill in or obscure any pyrographic detail. Try using watercolours in situations where you require more of a tint than a solid area of colour.

Fig 10.21 A close-up of the neck. The deeply-engraved feather outlines are a guide to the painting.

Fig 10.22 The completed cockerel, including the pyrographing of the beak and feet.

11
PYROGRAPHING
WOODTURNED OBJECTS

Working on non-flat surfaces is not as hard as you might think. Once you have attained a reasonable level of pyrographic dexterity, there is no reason why you should not attempt to engrave a bowl, rolling pin, egg cup or any other apparently awkward-shaped item. The most important requirement is to find a comfortable position for your hand as you work, so that the shape of the object does not affect the quality of your pyrography.

WORKING ON CURVED SURFACES

Rest the heel of your hand on a raised surface adjacent to and approximately level with the surface you want to pyrograph, so that the point of the pencil is within comfortable reach of the wood, as it would be when working on a flat surface. Your other hand can hold the handle or edge of the object, rotating it slowly as you progress with your design (see Fig 11.1).

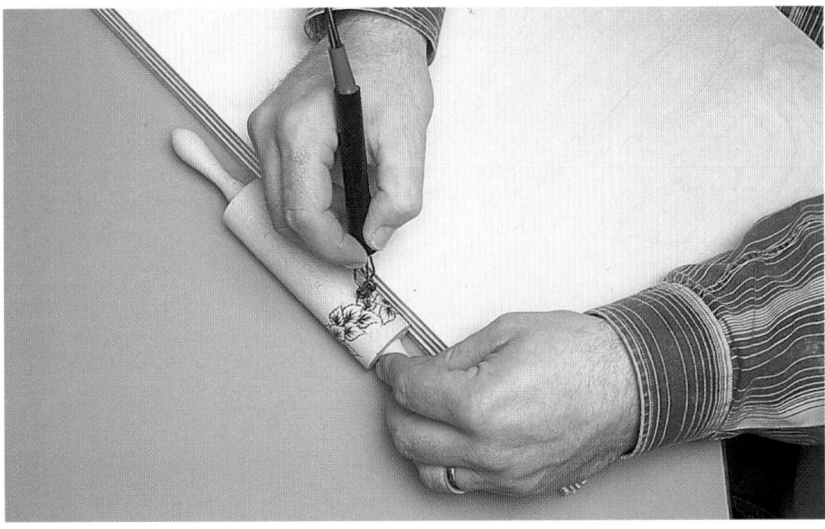

Fig 11.1 Pyrographing the design on a rolling pin. The hand is resting on a stack of ply sheets to bring it level with the surface that is being worked on.

PYROGRAPHING A BOWL

I used a sycamore pot pourri bowl manufactured by Janik, 8½in (216mm) in diameter and 2in (51mm) deep (see Fig 11.2). My design deliberately covers the more inaccessible parts of the bowl, partly to demonstrate that this kind of work is not that difficult and partly because these are the parts that will be on display. If the bowl is put to its intended use, then the pot pourri would cover any design pyrographed on the bottom.

Begin by making a stack of pieces of scrap wood or sheets of ply approximately the same height as the depth of the bowl. (You could also use a suitably thick hardback book for this, as long as it has sufficient surface area to rest your hand on comfortably.)

I wanted a bold, heavy design for the bowl, so opted to use a solid-point machine – the Janik G4, with four attachments (nos. 22, B21, B24 and 25).

TRACING THE DESIGN

Tracing a repeat design on a curved surface can cause minor difficulties. The secret is to use as a basis a design of a size that will sit *in* the curve, rather than around it. The focal point of my design is a simple drawing of a dog rose. The original line illustration was drawn approximately 1⅛in (28mm) across. Use the more traditional tracing technique of covering the reverse of the drawing with soft pencil carbon.

The first thing to do is mark the boundaries of your design on the

Fig 11.2 A sycamore pot pourri bowl 8½in (216mm) in diameter and 2in (51mm) deep, supplied by Janik.

rim and inside of the bowl. For the inside you will need a small plate, saucer or round lid that will sit inside the bowl, exposing only the area to be worked on. Hold the inverted bowl firmly in position, and mark a soft pencil line around it (see Fig 11.3). For the rim, build a stack of ply up to the desired level and, with the bowl butted up to the edge of the ply, place a soft pencil on top of the stack. Make sure that the pencil lead just overhangs the stack enough to touch the rim in

the position you need it, and then, holding the pencil in position with one hand, carefully rotate the bowl with the other hand until you have made a pencil line all the way round (see Fig 11.4). You can now trace on your flower design.

Cut out the photocopy of your chosen flower, leaving just enough white paper around it so it can be stuck with masking tape to the bowl. Don't leave too much – the larger the paper, the harder it is to work it round the curve. Attach it in

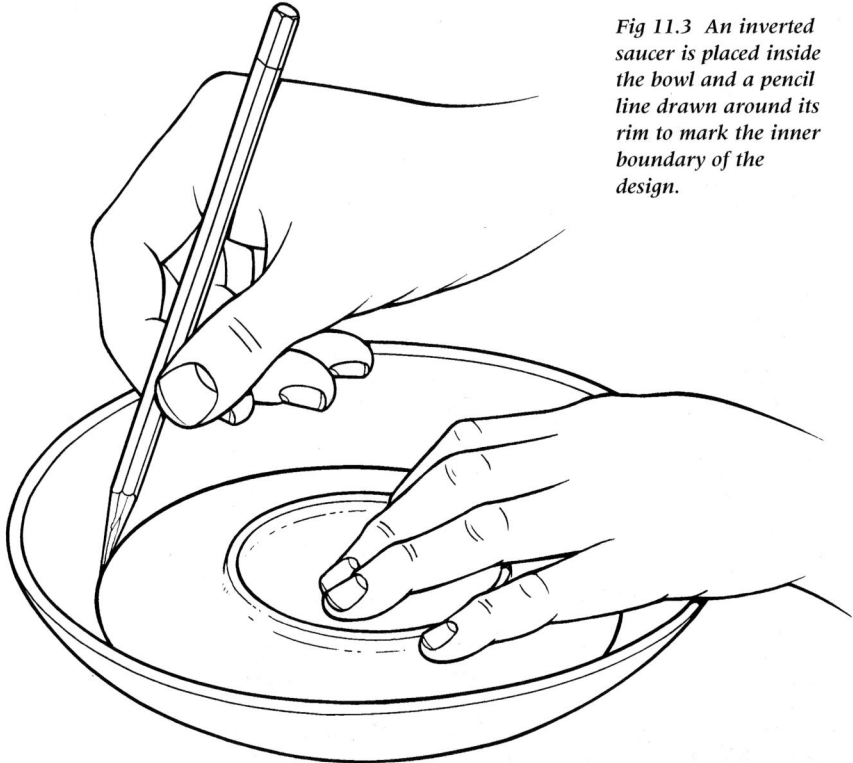

Fig 11.3 An inverted saucer is placed inside the bowl and a pencil line drawn around its rim to mark the inner boundary of the design.

this way at the top of the flower and the side. Then place a single piece of ply on your work surface and position the bowl on its rim against the far edge of the ply with the inside of the bowl facing you. The area to be worked on will now be an extension of the ply, providing that the thickness of the bowl rim is approximately equal to the thickness of the ply (see Fig 11.5).

I arranged my flowers in various positions; the calculations needed to make the design symmetrical could no doubt be made, but I preferred a freer design. You will notice that my flowers are placed in different rotations, and two of them have encroached inside the inner boundary. When working in this way, be careful to keep an eye on the spaces between these tracings. I deliberately spaced them unevenly, checking when I had three or four more to trace that I had a reasonable amount of room to fit the last two in, so as to keep the design balanced.

PYROGRAPHING THE LINES

Once the flowers are in place, pyrography can begin. I used a no. B21 point set at near-maximum temperature for the outlines. The only concern here is that some lines will be with the grain, others against it. Use some pressure and be positive, or else risk allowing the grain to dictate where the point will travel. Where one of the flowers appears inside the inner edge of the

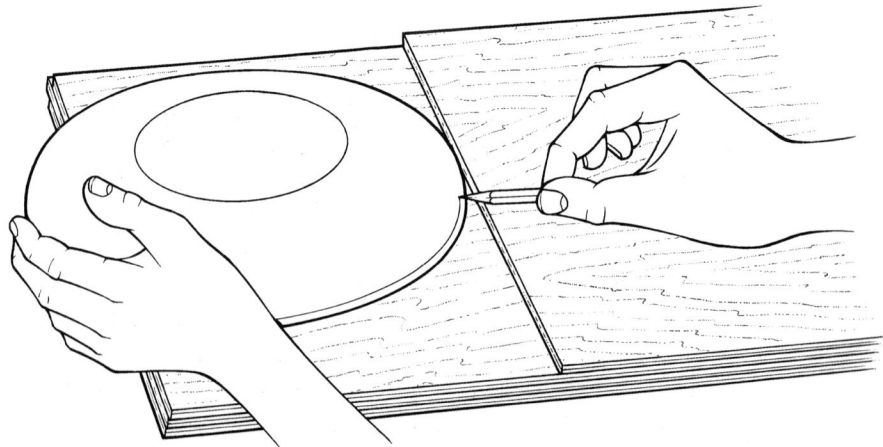

Fig 11.4 The inverted bowl is butted up to the edge of a short stack of ply, and a pencil overhanging the stack is used to draw a line at a point just below the rim. This marks the outer boundary of the design.

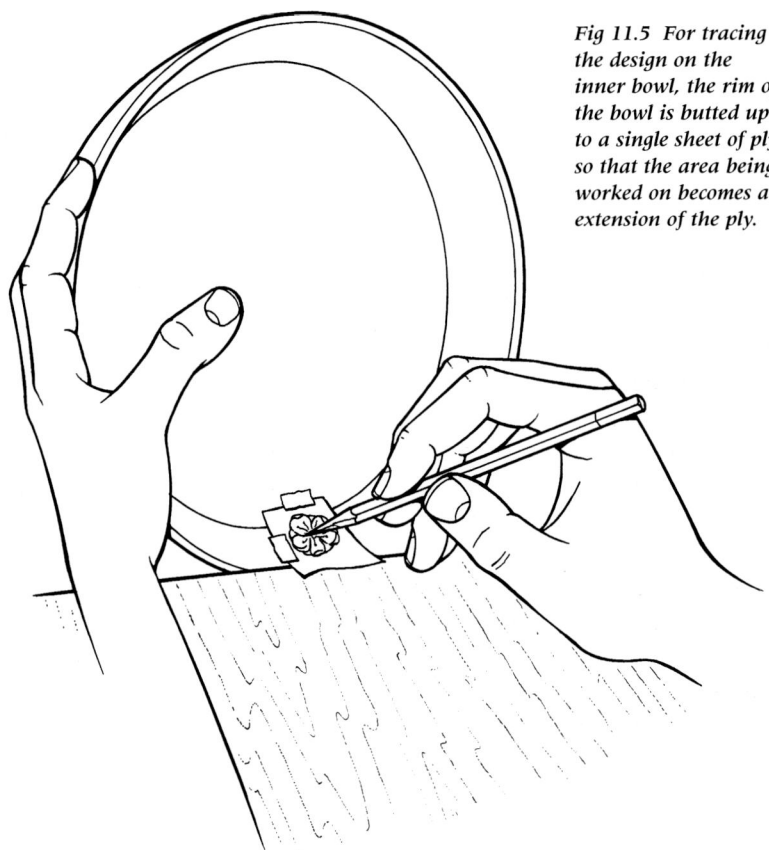

Fig 11.5 For tracing the design on the inner bowl, the rim of the bowl is butted up to a single sheet of ply so that the area being worked on becomes an extension of the ply.

design, it is easier to pyrograph it by reaching across it with the bowl standing normally. Where the petals have reached slightly onto the top of the rim, you need to make a stack of ply equal to the depth of the bowl and then place the bowl right-side up, butted up to the edge of the stack (see Fig 11.6). The bulk of the pyrographed petals can be produced by placing the bowl in the position described for the tracing (see page 104).

PYROGRAPHING THE BOUNDARIES

The rest of the pyrography involves the production of textures. I am always in favour of completing the more problematic sections early, thereby alleviating in part the risk of making a serious mistake towards the end. With this in mind, I marked in the lines at the edges of the design first, using a no. B24 point, set at maximum temperature.

The best way to position the bowl for this stage is to hold it rather like a discus, supported against your body with the work area on the edge of the table (see Fig 11.7). Again, a single sheet of ply will raise the level of the point and enable you to simulate working on a flat surface. Lean the bowl so it is angled slightly away from your pencil hand, and then gradually rotate it at intervals while carefully pyrographing a line of dots along the inner pencil line boundary. If a dot or two strays inside the line it will not matter, but be careful not to wander outside the line. You are aiming for a consistent and accurate set of marks.

To mark in a similar line on the outside of the bowl requires the construction of a simple ramp. Lean a single sheet of ply against an old hardback book. The hand holding the pyrography pencil should rest on the book, while the bowl is placed upside down on the ply (see Fig 11.8). It is important to direct the light from your lamp onto the area you are working, because you will have to work at a slight angle to the surface and a clear view is crucial if you are to follow the pencil guide accurately.

ADDING TEXTURE

Once the pencil lines have been covered, further similar work needs to be carried out to thicken them up. Work round the inside of the bowl and carefully put in the marks

Fig 11.6 To pyrograph the top of the rim, butt the bowl up to the edge of a stack of ply the same height as the bowl.

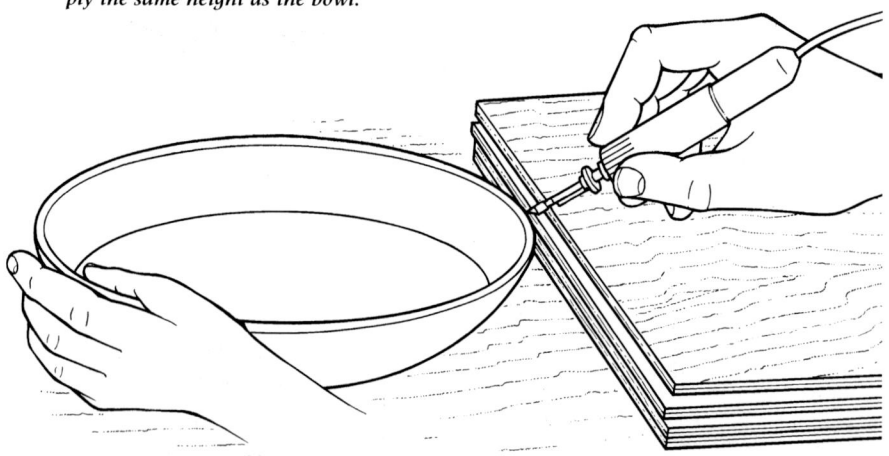

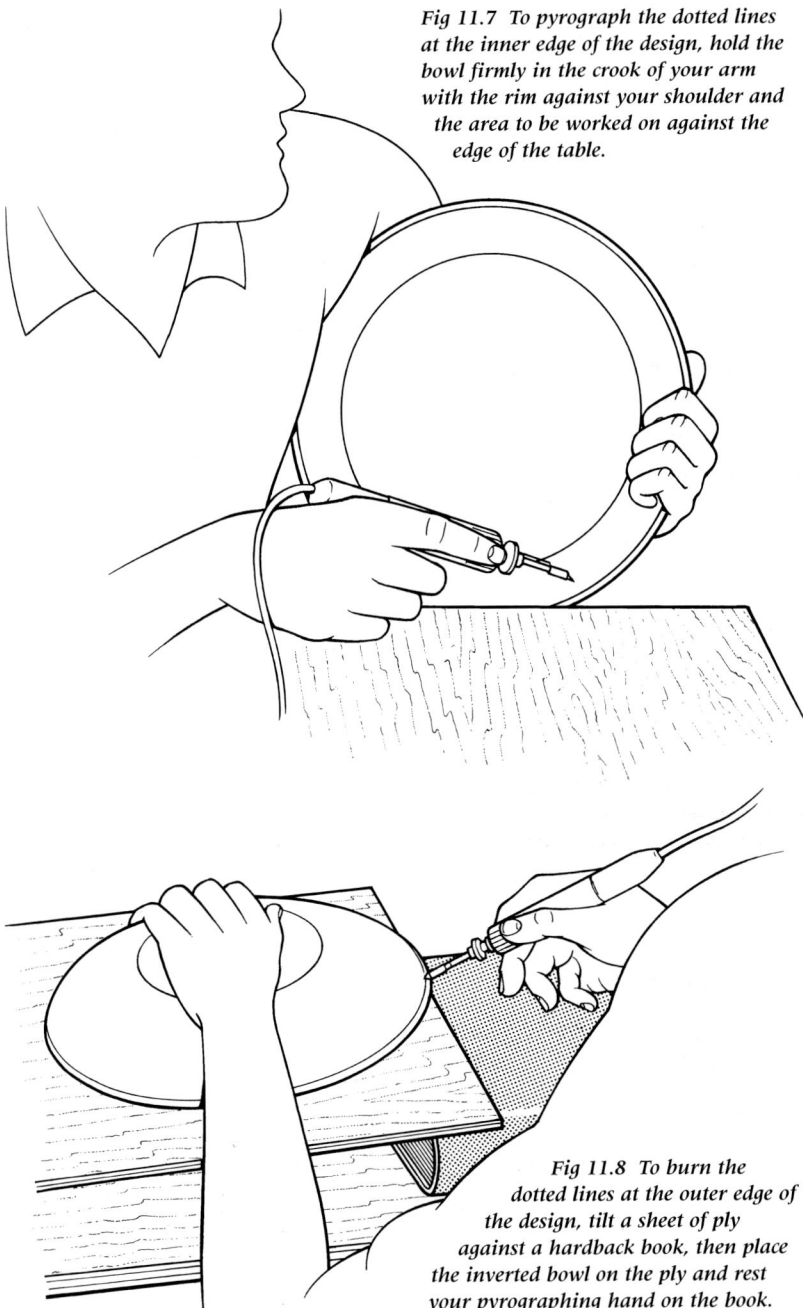

Fig 11.7 To pyrograph the dotted lines at the inner edge of the design, hold the bowl firmly in the crook of your arm with the rim against your shoulder and the area to be worked on against the edge of the table.

Fig 11.8 To burn the dotted lines at the outer edge of the design, tilt a sheet of ply against a hardback book, then place the inverted bowl on the ply and rest your pyrographing hand on the book.

outside the outline of the petals, slowly increasing the text-ured area to highlight the flowers within the rest of the design.

Use the cutting edge of the no. 25 point for the next texture, which is a simple matter of producing groups of cuts, usually four at a time. Work from the dark texture around each flower and similarly from the boundary line, leaving occasional gaps for the addition of the final texture. For this, revert to the B21 point, this time working more quickly to give darker, smaller marks along the top of the bowl's rim. To link up the small round marks to the groups of cut marks, and to cover the rim top, repeat this process but at a reduced temperature setting.

Finally, something is needed in the centres of the flowers. Take the no. 22 point and set it at maximum temperature. The centre of each flower is represented by a group of marks made by pushing the point vertically into the wood. The stamens were created using flick strokes with the same point, and these were punctuated with more vertically pyrographed marks.

12
ADVANCED PYROGRAPHY

You should by now have picked up the basic skills of the craft, so this chapter aims to stretch you a little with a more complex project, which incorporates all the skills you have learned so far, and some new ones.

PROJECT:
READING WAGON

Subjects involving any sort of timber construction nearly always produce good pyrography, and the design shown in Fig 12.1 came from a Romany book showing a breakdown of the way a Romany wagon is constructed, identifying all the extraneous parts. I used a sycamore rectangular plaque measuring 12$\frac{1}{2}$ x 8$\frac{1}{2}$in (317 x 216mm) for this piece, but you could equally well use birch-faced ply or a veneer.

TRACING THE ORIGINAL

Take a photocopy of the drawings to the size you require. I made my photocopy so that the wagon was approximately 5$\frac{1}{2}$in (140mm) long from the shaft ends to the steps. Cut out the wagon, leaving enough

of a border to enable you to attach the photocopy to the wood. Have Fig 12.1 to hand (or a copy of it) to help identify the parts of the wagon.

Now trace through the copy and pencil carbon underneath (see Fig 12.2). Don't worry about large shadow areas at this stage; concentrate on the main lines and marks. Don't insert any extra detail – the time to enhance the work will come later. Before removing the original, check carefully that nothing has been missed. You may wish to leave the copy stuck to the wood by one edge, so that it can be folded back over the pyrograph now and again as you work to check everything is in place.

PYROGRAPHING THE LINES

Set the wire point to a temperature that will allow you to apply reasonable pressure without overburning. You want to burn only the traced lines at this stage, removing as much as possible of the carbon lines (see Fig 12.3).

This kind of pyrography – like any form of engraving – restricts you to working on very small areas

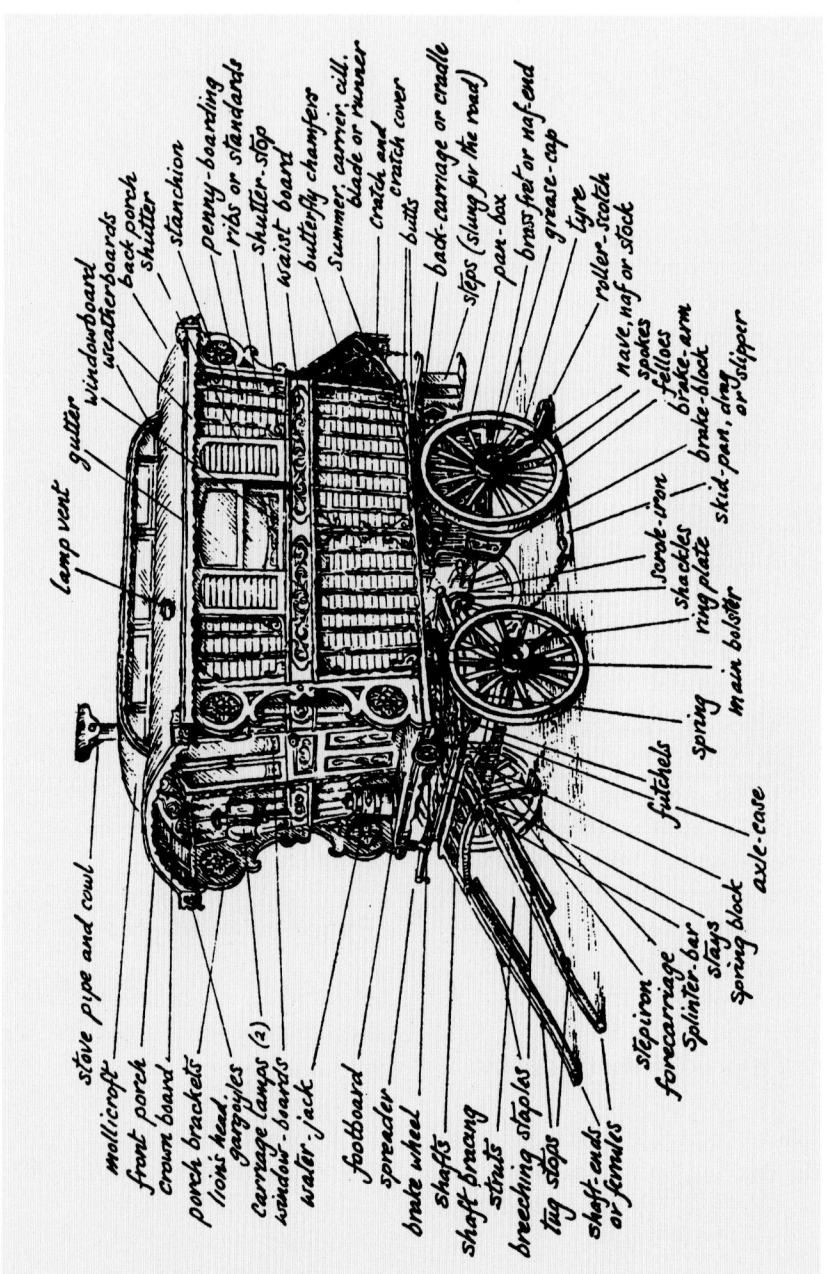

Fig 12.1 Romany wagon template.

Fig 12.2 The main lines and marks from the drawing transferred to the sycamore.

Fig 12.3 The line pyrography begun.

at a time. Start at a point where there are a few simple lines grouped together. Work slowly and carefully on that area, and then move on to the next, and so on. Have patience, take your time, and of course do a few practice runs on a piece of scrap wood to build up your confidence. Continue until the whole tracing is pyrographed (see Fig 12.4).

BEGINNING THE SHADING

Refer back to the original and take some time to study where the lines are thicker or weightier. There should be no need to adjust the temperature setting; darker lines and marks can be achieved by using a little more pressure and working a little slower. In Fig 12.1, the artist has suggested decorative carving on many of the boards and brackets of the wagon without actually supplying any detail. If you burn straight lines, and ignore this suggestion of carving, the visual flavour of the subject will be lost. Study the strut running along the bottom of the side of the wagon. This clearly shows sections that have been neatly carved out of the wood. It is fair to assume that the ribs (known as 'standards')

Fig 12.4 The line pyrography completed.

running vertically over the horizontal penny boarding would have been decoratively carved in the same way. When you were tracing and then burning away the trace lines, you probably showed all these as straight lines.

As you study the piece and burn in the thicker lines, the pyrograph will begin to come to life (see Fig 12.5). Don't worry about large areas of shadow at this stage, but fill in all the smaller solid lines and areas. Treat the wheels in this way, and also the little areas that denote the undercarriage. A lot of detail under the wagon is not clear,

and the finished pyrograph will show this area in shadow, so don't worry about it.

If you had a go at the hinge design in Chapter 9 you will understand how careful shading can give life to a piece of pyrography. Take your time and look very carefully to see where the small dark lines and areas of minute dark shading can collectively enhance the overall effect.

The shutters on either side of the window are constructed from angled overlapping boards to admit air and exclude rain when closed. Intermittent shading down each side

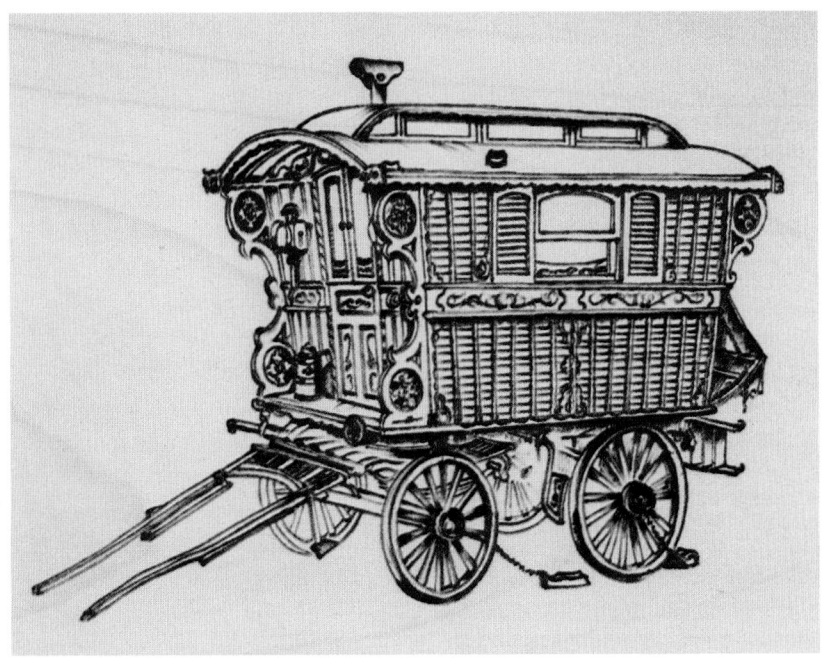

Fig 12.5 The thicker lines burned in.

Fig 12.6 The roof of the wagon pyrographed to suggest the curves and texture of the original.

of the shutters is a simple way of showing their construction.

At the front of the wagon there are many small areas, such as directly under the crown boards of the front porch, the lamp, behind the water jack and under the footboard, that all require carefully and slowly pyrographed dark lines – the darker the better.

SHADING WITH THE WIRE POINT

You may find some of the very smallest areas are easier to shade using the wire point, such as the dark area below the weatherboard directly above the side window. The dark shading here clearly shows the

shape of the bottom of the weatherboard. The shading was achieved by using the wire point, slowly and with a fair amount of pressure, to burn a dark line along the bottom of the weatherboard to form a groove. Then work vertically with short strokes, from the groove downwards. When you reach the top of the shutters there is very little room to shade comfortably with anything other than the wire point.

The main roof and the mollicroft, whether made from stretched fabric or shaped wooden boards, have a texture that can easily be suggested using the wire point.

Use a lower temperature setting and pyrograph a series of touching lines following the curves already suggested in the drawing. Use plenty of pressure to obtain the textured effect (see Fig 12.6). Before you attempt this, practise on a piece of scrap wood and be sure of the technique. You are now well into this piece of pyrography, and it is common at this point to be tempted to speed up the work. This can result in the application of a point that is too hot, resulting in disaster, so beware!

The trickiest section in this project is the delicate shading that represents the glass in the window. Again this is best done with the wire point, but at an even lower temperature setting. As you can see, it is just a series of angled lines.

However, be very careful not to use excess pressure. Try to denote a suggestion of reflection, rather than texture.

SHADING WITH THE SPOON POINT

The advantage of the spoon point is that, if used correctly, it can produce hard, rigid lines (such as those in the blackberry design on page 74), and subtler, gentler untextured shading. It is the latter that is needed on the wagon. Do some practice first. Set the temperature low, so that you can produce small, lightly shaded areas of approximately ¼in (6mm) square. Aim for a colour

Fig 12.7 Further shading done on the side of the wagon, extending the shadow areas with graduated tones.

of shading similar to that achieved with the wire point on the roof of the wagon.

Now you can begin to add the final touches to the shading. Start with the side of the wagon, gently continuing with the various areas begun darkly with the point to give a more extended and gradual area of tone (see Fig 12.7). Make constant reference to the original as you go along.

As mentioned, the underside of the wagon is a gloomy area filled with shadows and hence requires little detail. Use the spoon point to shade the two dark patches between the tops of the wheels and the base of the wagon, using slow, deliberate strokes starting from the base, and reducing pressure while increasing speed as you progress between the wheels (see Fig 12.8).

At this stage you will find yourself working on the whole piece at once, adding little touches here and there, softening the rough edges of sharp lines created by the shading work done with the wire point. It is the time to add a lot of shading detail to the front porch, which is the focal point of the work. Other sections to pay particular attention to are the wooden panels, the inside of the porch bracket and the waist boards, all of which will benefit from careful shading (see Fig 12.9).

Fig 12.8 One of the darker areas beneath the wagon burned in using the spoon point.

Fig 12.9 Detail showing the porch of the wagon, with its various features shaded.

USING THE GRAIN MARKINGS

To finish off the project, try using the natural grain markings to your advantage. So that the wagon doesn't look as if it's floating in mid air, add some landscape detail, to suggest earth, stones and weeds. The important thing to notice on my example in Fig 12.10, is that certain grain lines have been followed, and in fact provide the basis for the background and foreground. Where the grain lines appear to move away behind the wagon I toned down the effect. You will find this a simple and very effective way of giving the work depth.

Fig 12.10 The grain lines of the sycamore were followed when I pyrographed the background and foreground, thereby giving the work depth.

13
PROTECTING THE FINISHED PYROGRAPH

Unless your work is going to be framed behind glass, then some protection such as a varnish or a polish will be necessary. Pyrographs that are likely to be handled frequently, such as boxes or key-fobs, are especially vulnerable to wear. Another hazard is direct sunlight. Over a prolonged period, exposure to sunlight tends to cause most wood surfaces to darken slightly. At the same time, the ultra-violet rays contained within sunlight will eventually reduce the density of finely burned lines and marks. Applying a finish to your pyrograph as soon as it is complete will go some way to reducing these effects.

TYPES OF FINISH

For a good gloss finish, I recommend any sort of polyurethane varnish; yacht varnish is particularly hard wearing. Apply as many coats as your patience allows; the more coats,

Fig 13.1 These key-rings were finished with a polyurethane varnish.

the deeper the shine.

For a polished finish, apply two coats of any acrylic varnish (preferably clear satin). Acrylic varnish has the advantage of being very quick drying and water soluble, so you can wash your brushes in water. When completely dry, smooth the surface very gently with very fine wire wool and solid furniture polish. After the second application of furniture polish, simply polish with a soft cloth.

FINISHING HINTS

▌ Ensure the wood surface is perfectly smooth. Varnish always accentuates scratches and blemishes.

▌ Always apply several thin coats of varnish or polish, not one or two thicker coats.

▌ Only use the finest grade of wire wool available.

▌ I have found the best results are obtained by applying the finish using make-up brushes, as they don't leave brush marks.

▌ If you need to finish a piece very quickly, you can use several thin coats of car lacquer, applied from an aerosol. The result will be satisfactory, but not as good, lacking as it does the level of control that brushes allow.

TEMPLATES

ABOUT THE AUTHOR

Stephen Poole was born in Buckinghamshire in 1948. The son of a maths teacher, he was rapidly frightened off numbers, and opted for a more creative direction at the Windsor Grammar School and the Berkshire College of Art, where he studied graphic design.

Since 1975, Stephen has spent time developing his own particular pyrography techniques, latterly running courses to pass on his adopted craft to others.

INDEX

BOOKS

WOODWORKING

40 More Woodworking Plans & Projects	GMC Publications
Bird Boxes and Feeders for the Garden	Dave Mackenzie
Complete Woodfinishing	Ian Hosker
Electric Woodwork	Jeremy Broun
Furniture & Cabinetmaking Projects	GMC Publications
Furniture Projects	Rod Wales
Furniture Restoration (Practical Crafts)	Kevin Jan Bonner
Furniture Restoration and Repair for Beginners	Kevin Jan Bonner
Green Woodwork	Mike Abbott
The Incredible Router	Jeremy Broun
Making & Modifying Woodworking Tools	Jim Kingshott
Making Chairs and Tables	GMC Publications
Making Fine Furniture	Tom Darby
Making Little Boxes from Wood	John Bennett
Making Shaker Furniture	Barry Jackson
Pine Furniture Projects for the Home	Dave Mackenzie
Routing for Beginners	Anthony Bailey
Sharpening Pocket Reference Book	Jim Kingshott
Sharpening: The Complete Guide	Jim Kingshott
Space-Saving Furniture Projects	Dave Mackenzie
Stickmaking: A Complete Course	Andrew Jones & Clive George
Test Reports: *The Router* and *Furniture & Cabinetmaking*	GMC Publications
Veneering: A Complete Course	Ian Hosker
Woodfinishing Handbook (Practical Crafts)	Ian Hosker
Woodworking Plans and Projects	GMC Publications
The Workshop	Jim Kingshott

WOODTURNING

Adventures in Woodturning	David Springett
Bert Marsh: Woodturner	Bert Marsh
Bill Jones' Notes from the Turning Shop	Bill Jones
Bill Jones' Further Notes from the Turning Shop	Bill Jones
Colouring Techniques for Woodturners	Jan Sanders
The Craftsman Woodturner	Peter Child
Decorative Techniques for Woodturners	Hilary Bowen
Essential Tips for Woodturners	GMC Publications
Faceplate Turning	GMC Publications
Fun at the Lathe	R.C. Bell
Illustrated Woodturning Techniques	John Hunnex
Intermediate Woodturning Projects	GMC Publications
Keith Rowley's Woodturning Projects	Keith Rowley
Make Money from Woodturning	Ann & Bob Phillips
Multi-Centre Woodturning	Ray Hopper
Pleasure and Profit from Woodturning	Reg Sherwin
Practical Tips for Turners & Carvers	GMC Publications
Practical Tips for Woodturners	GMC Publications

Spindle Turning	GMC Publications
Turning Miniatures in Wood	John Sainsbury
Turning Wooden Toys	Terry Lawrence
Understanding Woodturning	Ann & Bob Phillips
Useful Techniques for Woodturners	GMC Publications
Useful Woodturning Projects	GMC Publications
Woodturning: Bowls, Platters, Hollow Forms, Vases, Vessels, Bottles, Flasks, Tankards, Plates	GMC Publications
Woodturning: A Foundation Course	Keith Rowley
Woodturning: A Source Book of Shapes	John Hunnex
Woodturning Jewellery	Hilary Bowen
Woodturning Masterclass	Tony Boase
Woodturning Techniques	GMC Publications
Woodturning Tools & Equipment Test Reports	GMC Publications
Woodturning Wizardry	David Springett

WOODCARVING

The Art of the Woodcarver	GMC Publications
Carving Birds & Beasts	GMC Publications
Carving on Turning	Chris Pye
Carving Realistic Birds	David Tippey
Decorative Woodcarving	Jeremy Williams
Essential Tips for Woodcarvers	GMC Publications
Essential Woodcarving Techniques	Dick Onians
Lettercarving in Wood: A Practical Course	Chris Pye
Power Tools for Woodcarving	David Tippey
Practical Tips for Turners & Carvers	GMC Publications
Relief Carving in Wood: A Practical Introduction	Chris Pye
Understanding Woodcarving	GMC Publications
Understanding Woodcarving in the Round	GMC Publications
Useful Techniques for Woodcarvers	GMC Publications
Wildfowl Carving – Volume 1	Jim Pearce
Wildfowl Carving – Volume 2	Jim Pearce
The Woodcarvers	GMC Publications
Woodcarving: A Complete Course	Ron Butterfield
Woodcarving: A Foundation Course	Zoë Gertner
Woodcarving for Beginners	GMC Publications
Woodcarving Tools & Equipment Test Reports	GMC Publications
Woodcarving Tools, Materials & Equipment	Chris Pye

UPHOLSTERY

Seat Weaving (Practical Crafts)	Ricky Holdstock
Upholsterer's Pocket Reference Book	David James
Upholstery: A Complete Course	David James
Upholstery Restoration	David James
Upholstery Techniques & Projects	David James

TOYMAKING

Designing & Making Wooden Toys	Terry Kelly
Fun to Make Wooden Toys & Games	Jeff & Jennie Loader
Making Board, Peg & Dice Games	Jeff & Jennie Loader
Making Wooden Toys & Games	Jeff & Jennie Loader
Restoring Rocking Horses	Clive Green & Anthony Dew

MAGAZINES

WOODTURNING • WOODCARVING • FURNITURE & CABINETMAKING
THE DOLLS' HOUSE MAGAZINE • CREATIVE CRAFTS FOR THE HOME
THE ROUTER • THE SCROLLSAW • BUSINESSMATTERS

The above represents a full list of all titles currently published or scheduled to be published.
All are available direct from the Publishers or through bookshops, newsagents and specialist retailers.
To place an order, or to obtain a complete catalogue, contact:

GMC Publications,
Castle Place, 166 High Street, Lewes, East Sussex BN7 1XU, United Kingdom
Tel: 01273 488005 Fax: 01273 478606

Orders by credit card are accepted